CONTEMPORARY INTERIORS A SOURCE OF DESIGN IDEAS

First published in the United States of America
in 2016 by
Rizzoli International Publications, Inc.
300 Park Avenue South
New York, NY 10010
www.rizzoliusa.com

Editor: Ellen R. Cohen

Designed by MGMT. design

ISBN: 978-0-8478-4804-1
Library of Congress Control Number: 2015952714

Printed in China

2016 2017 2018 2019 2020 / 10 9 8 7 6 5 4 3 2 1

Photograph Credits

David Adjaye: 20, 22, 23; Tadao Ando (Architect & Associates): 24, 26, 29; Iwan Baan Studio: 9, 66, 68–71, 76, 78–83, 84, 86–89, 90, 92–95, 154, 156–61, 190, 192–95, 254, 256–59; Shigeru Ban Architects: 40, 42–45; Bruce Buck: 182, 184, 185; Ehrlich Architects: 46, 48–51; Ferrater Architects/ Alejo Bague: 16–17, 58, 60–65; Leonardo Finotti: 14–15, 122, 124–27, 238, 240–43; Scott Frances/OTTO: 134, 136–41; Sean Godsell Architects: 72, 74, 75; Roland Halbe Fotografie: 10, 30, 32–35, 36, 38, 39, 52, 54–57, 96, 98–103 104, 106–109, 142, 144, 145, 166, 168–71, 172, 174–77; Patrick Jouin: 96, 98–103; Lussi + Halter: 110, 112–15; MADA Spam/Baan: 116, 118–21; Peter Marino: 128,130–33; Shelton Mindel/ Michael Moran: 146, 148, 149; Michael Moran/ OTTO: 150, 152, 153; Sergio Pirrone: 244, 246–49, 290, 292–95, 296, 289–301; Richard Powers: 272, 274–79; Roman and Williams: 178, 180, 181, 186, 188, 189; Glenn Sestig Architects: 196, 198, 199, 200, 202–205; Shim-Sutcliffe Architects: 18–19, 228, 230–233, 234, 236, 237; Álvaro Siza/Roland Halbe: 206, 208–211; Werner Sobek: 212, 214, 215, 216, 218, 219; Studio Mumbai: 220, 222–27; UN Studio: 250, 252, 253; Paul Warchol: 162, 164, 165; Isay Weinfeld: 6, 260, 262–65, 266, 268–71; Jean-Michel Wilmotte: 280, 282–85, 286, 288–89

CONTEMPORARY INTERIORS A SOURCE OF DESIGN IDEAS

PHILIP JODIDIO

New York · Paris · London · Milan

CONTENTS

DAS REICH

FROM THE OUTSIDE LOOKING IN CONTEMPORARY INTERIORS

How do other people live? Residential interiors are normally private spaces, but this is a book that shows them to all. Such a publication may serve as a source for those who wish to create their own space, or perhaps it may satisfy voyeuristic curiosity. Of course these are not "ordinary" interiors; they are meant to be exceptional, whether for reasons of their design, or because of the choice of furnishings and objects, or simply because of the proximity to nature that they afford. On the other hand, interiors, particularly in their most private spaces, are also meant to be protected places. "The house," states the Swiss architect Mario Botta, "is intimately related to the idea of shelter. A cave carved out of the rock is like a mother's womb. This is the concept of the house that I defend. When I am tired of the world, I want to go home. There I can regain my energy to prepare for the next day's battle. As long as there is a man who needs a house, architecture will still exist. . . . A house should be like a mother's womb."[1]

FUNDAMENTAL CHANGES

Interiors are more than a matter of style. They reflect the personalities of the designers, owners, and architects who form them, but they are also a barometer of sweeping societal changes. A 1999 exhibition at New York's Museum of Modern Art entitled *The Un-Private House* sought to define the ways in which the home adapts to the way people live. Terence Riley, then chief curator at MoMA's Department of Architecture and Design, wrote, "There have been fundamental changes in all of the aspects that constitute the private house, changes in the family, changes in the relationship between the house and work. For several centuries, the way one defined the private house was by the absence of work. There have been changes in the notion of domesticity; changes in the notion of privacy itself."[2] Instead of distinct living and dining rooms, houses are now more likely to be divided into what architects call "public" and "private" space, even if few interiors are really "public." Recomposed families are more the norm than the exception, and this too has consequences on the interior organization of residences. Another marked tendency, seen in a number of the residences published here, like the Daeyang House (Seoul, South Korea, 2012), by Steven Holl, has been to combine essentially public spaces, intended for the exhibition of art, with a "private" home. This is also very much the case with the Tsai Residence and Studio (Ancram, New York, 2008/2011), by the Swiss-based architects HHF, working in collaboration with the noted Chinese artist Ai Weiwei.

A number of Japanese architects, like Sou Fujimoto, have been experimenting in recent years with houses that are entirely open, without clearly defined floor levels and a great deal of what might be called "intermediate space" (House K, Nishinomiya, Japan, 2012). It is tempting to draw a parallel between this type of design and the way we use the Internet. Although there are "pages," as in books, hyperlinks allow navigation that is no longer linear. One can jump from one subject or one site to another. Similarly, inside a house, there may well be a desire to create spaces that one can jump to and use as one pleases, no longer defined in a strict hierarchical order, able to be transformed according to their current function.

ROOMS WITH A VIEW

It may well be that one of the most significant recent developments in residential interiors has been an increase in the importance of views, or in the dissolution of the boundaries between interior and exterior. Depending on circumstances, these two approaches—a view through a window or an operable glass door—can be seen as opposites. Niklas Maak, writing in the context of the 2014 Venice Architecture Biennale, asks, "But what are we talking about when we talk about 'private' and 'public' spheres? . . . As a pair of conceptual opposites, inside and outside, once separated by walls, connected by doors and windows, have lost much of their usefulness, if they ever had any. The glazed façade is always a physical partition, its openness to the world only an aesthetic gesture; it fictionalizes the world beyond. A counter model would be the traditional Japanese house, with its sliding doors that could selectively open up the building physically at the *engawa*, the porch-like space between the house and garden."[3]

A large number of the residences published in this volume do have considerable glazed areas that can be entirely opened to the exterior. This is naturally much more frequent in warm climates, as is the case with the spectacular YTL Residence (Kuala Lumpur, Malaysia, 2008), by the Paris designers Jouin Manku, or the houses in Latin America by Isay Weinfeld, Mathias Klotz, or WMR. On the other hand, broad views of natural surroundings are also part of interior designs in less inviting climates, for example, in Shim-Sutcliffe's Integral House (Toronto, Canada, 2009). It may be this type of design that inspired Rem Koolhaas, director of the 2014 Venice Architecture Biennale, to comment, "Fewer and fewer windows can be opened, offering enormous uninterrupted views of the world, but no physical contact with it."[4]

FROM DESIGN TO ARCHITECTURE

A distinction has traditionally been made between architecture and interior design, although in most of the cases published here, both are of interest. In fact, numerous designers featured in this book formed their reputations in the area of interiors and have since made the logical step to building more and more new structures from the ground up. This is true of Peter Marino, well known in the United States, or of Jean-Michel Wilmotte, designer of the interiors of a substantial part of the Louvre and the Rijksmuseum in Amsterdam. Wilmotte started as a furniture designer and went on to create urban furniture for the Champs-Élysées in Paris, for example, but also to renovate often prestigious old buildings. His two projects published here, a grand eighteenth-century town house in Lyon and the Jean-Pierre Raynaud Atelier in Barbizon, France, are both renovation projects, but they include new spaces and architectural elements that go well beyond what might traditionally be called "decoration."

Another interesting case of a movement from interior design to architecture is the 211 Elizabeth Street project (New York, 2009), by Roman and Williams. This is a seven-story new-build condominium located in the Nolita area of Manhattan, at the corner of Prince Street. With its brick façades, the building looks much older than it is. Firm principal Stephen Alesch explains, "It seems things took a detour for a long time into convenient construction and easy ways out. We see this as a continuation of, say, the period prior to the Great Depression, before beefy, strong, solid American architecture lost its way." The suggestion that American architecture may have "lost its way" in this context may imply a certain rejection of the modernist heritage, which is all well and good. In fact, a voluntary aspect of this book is that very "modern" houses like Tadao Ando's House in Monterrey (Monterrey, Mexico, 2011) are juxtaposed with more "traditional" interiors like that of the Brooklyn Town House (Brooklyn, New York, 2013), also by Roman and Williams. In this instance, the designers were asked to do away with the formerly "modern and minimalist design style" of the interiors to return to "a more textured, layered aesthetic hearkening back to the home's roots." Is the result of their work an expression of nostalgia? Objects selected for the interiors include a Berber carpet, a buffalo hide draped over a black leather sofa, an 1850s Indian four-poster bed, a Louis XVI daybed, and a vintage Aubusson rug. One might venture to say that what brings together such an interior with those of Tadao Ando is the real spirit of the times, which is to say eclecticism. Collectors of the past (and some of the present) have focused on a given period or type of object. Today, however, not only the accessibility of objects from all over the world, but also the mentality of designers and owners allow for great variety in the choice of objects. "Globalization" is a term usually applied to industrial and economic matters, but it also applies to interiors. The whole world and its objects are available to those with the taste or discernment to juxtapose pieces that may have been conceived by different civilizations centuries and thousands of miles apart.

LOOKING FOR THE SOUL

Other interiors published here attempt to place an emphasis only on the present, as might be the case with Cloudline (Columbia County, New York, 2011), by Toshiko Mori, a private residence with view of the countryside. Another dealer, Houssein Jarouche, the founder of the Brazilian design store MiCasa, called on the architects Triptyque for his São Paulo apartment. Rough concrete surfaces, reclaimed wood floors, and white walls offer an intentionally neutral background for colorful design works by the likes of Patricia Urquiola and Konstantin Grcic, Jarouche's stock in trade. It does happen, of course, that architect-designed interiors remain cold and impersonal, but in this case, Jarouche says, "The truth is that at my place I do not combine art pieces with furniture or other objects. I'm not interested if they are good or bad or beautiful; they just have to mean something to me. So everything happens in a natural way."[5]

The same possibility of coldness can also exist in numerous interiors where the emphasis is on something closer to decoration. Shelton, Mindel & Associates in New York successfully bridge the potential gap between architecture and interior design with such works as their Georgica Pond Residence (East Hampton, New York, 2007), based on the renovation of a modernist-style wooden house dating from the late 1970s. Interior walls in cedar and terra-cotta tiling on the floors were reconditioned but not replaced. Furniture was chosen in careful harmony with the forms of the house. Peter Shelton stated, "We tried to accept the building and embrace what it had to offer. The question was how to honor the old while bringing it forward."[6] The result is what the designers call a "seamless integration of architecture and interior design" that clearly did not lose the "soul" of the old house when it was rendered usable for today. What does connect the interiors published in this book, many designed by architects, is the relation between exterior and interior. We may venture to state that the most successful interiors are those with an intimate relationship to the architecture that they are part of.

WHITENESS & LIGHTNESS

Well known from the time of his earliest private houses for wanting to control not only exterior forms but also interiors, Richard Meier continues to build residences. His Fire Island House (Fire Island, New York, 2013) is set on the beach at Fair Harbor. Double-height curtain walls on three sides mark the oceanfront façades, allowing a flood of light into the typically white interiors. As he says, the "emphasis [is] on lightness and transparency; glass, wood and white finishes reflect the natural colors and beauty of the surrounding bay." It was a house somewhat like this one that prompted the author Tom Wolfe to write, in 1981, "Every new $900,000 summer house in the north woods of Michigan or on the shore of Long Island has so many pipe railings, ramps, hob-tread metal spiral stairways, sheets of industrial plate glass, banks of tungsten-halogen lamps, and white cylindrical shapes, it looks like an insecticide refinery. I once saw the owners of such a place driven to the edge of sensory deprivation by the whiteness & lightness & leanness & cleanness & bareness & spareness of it all. They became desperate for an antidote, such as coziness & color."[7] Wolfe's point is, of course, well taken by many who prefer "coziness and color" to whiteness, but Meier's concept does involve a proximity to nature in the form of daylight and views. His architecture and interiors can be said to completely oppose nature or—on the contrary, to accept it in its purest (white) forms. This is ultimately a matter of taste, whether a client prefers Berber rugs or aluminum panels, inclusive eclecticism or minimalist modernity; as seen in the interiors published here, both must be accepted as contemporary.

A more thoroughly contemporary example of the intimate relationship an architect can create between interior and exterior is the Haus am Weinberg (Stuttgart, Germany, 2011), by UNStudio. Architect Ben van Berkel challenges assumptions about the relationship between public and private space at the same time as he deals with the very different views from various parts of the house. His response involves "twisting" the forms so that public and private, interior and exterior, overlap while forming a whole. The architects give one example of this continuity, or "twisting," of the design: "A white kitchen table/work surface extends from the kitchen to the garden terrace, mimicking the curves in the architecture and further accentuating the connection between the inside and the outside." Van Berkel also juxtaposes his own penchant for computer-driven design with materials such as natural oak flooring, natural stone, and white clay stucco walls.

WELCOME TO MY CAVE

Mario Botta's comparison of the house to a cave or maternal womb has some relevance to a number of the projects published here. The Edward Street House (Melbourne, Australia, 2011), by Sean Godsell, is located in a "tough" part of the city and is enclosed in a galvanized steel shell, a kind of contemporary armor for a house whose largely wooden interiors are warm and comfortable in contrast. The Villa Vals (Vals, Switzerland, 2009), by the Dutch architects SeARCH, is almost the prototype of a modern cavelike residence. Located on the same hillside as Peter Zumthor's celebrated thermal baths (Therme Vals, 1996), this new house is inserted into the hillside in such a way as to render it nearly invisible from the baths. With a stone façade, the house makes no attempt to challenge the architectural "superiority" of its prestigious neighbor, creating instead a cavelike interior that characterizes its real presence.

Kulapat Yantrasast, a long-time collaborator of Tadao Ando, built his own residence not far from the beach in Venice, California (Venice House, 2012). The largely concrete structure assumes a cavelike form in its main living space, but it opens almost entirely to a central swimming pool. It is even possible to jump from an upper level of the house directly into the pool. Although calling on a mineral atmosphere that surely evokes much more ancient residences, the Venice House is both open and urban, taking in street noises and doing away with any separation between the outdoor pool and the indoors. This hierarchical upheaval again occurs in a climate where it is possible to open windows broadly most of the year, yet it also indicates new ways of perceiving the boundaries between inside and out, between the interior and the broader environment.

ENERGY SAVERS

Another designer who leans toward a rather minimalist approach is the German Werner Sobek, who has completed a number of energy-efficient houses, such as the D10 residence (Biberach an der Riss, Germany, 2010). In a design reminiscent of houses by Ludwig Mies van der Rohe, D10 incorporates such features as an efficient heat pump and photovoltaic cells that occupy the entire surface of the flat roof. With its simple alternation of fully glazed surfaces and opaque walls, the house is little more than a sophisticated modernist box, but its interior simplicity takes into account its energy concept. Though this house is surely not one built to "minimum" standards of space and luxury, it is stripped down to its ecological minimum. In this sense, the interiors, whose glass walls encourage a feeling of living in a site as opposed to occupying it, constitute a statement about architecture and design that goes beyond aesthetics to question the house in a more fundamental way. Equally ecological, but at the technological opposite of the D10 project, the Palmyra House (Nandgaon, India, 2007), by Studio Mumbai, is a two-story weekend home located in a coconut grove. Making use of local materials and building traditions, the house is largely open to the exterior as the climate permits. Three artesian wells provide water, and the design makes full use of natural ventilation and louvers for shade. Perhaps less overtly demonstrative in its ecological bias, the Palmyra House nonetheless is a model in terms of the coherence between interiors and exteriors, and between architecture and responsibility.

THE WAYS PEOPLE LIVE

Many of the residential interiors published here have involved very substantial budgets, and yet it may be that the interiors that most make one dream are not of that sort. The young Chilean firm WMR has completed a large number of residences along the Pacific coast. Their recently completed A residence is a tiny (344-square-foot/32-square-meter) pine and glass structure that sits above its wooded site, looking out to the ocean. This "super-low-cost" house blends interior and exterior into a whole and creates a place for relaxation or contemplation. More a nest set up on wooden scaffolding than a cave or safe haven, this is an interior that offers a view of the edge of the world.

There are more solutions for interiors than there are architects and designers in the world. Ideally, inside and out must be in harmony, but perhaps the most important element of any interior is that it must have a soul. Like the life in the eyes of a five-century-old portrait by Rembrandt, this soul is difficult to define; it is something that one must feel. Whether it is imparted by an architect or designer, or by a client, this soul is vibrant and present, by a light that radiates from within. At once private, even as they are rendered public in a book, these interiors are willfully eclectic; from minimalist white to cozy color, they are an image formed in just the past few years of the ways people live.

PHILIP JODIDIO
GRIMENTZ, SWITZERLAND
SEPTEMBER 2014

1

Silverlight

Architects **David Adjaye**
Location **London, United Kingdom** Year **2009**

This large house was designed for a narrow plot of land located along the Grand Union Canal in West London. The forms and cladding of the building were developed in response to the location, which includes a heavily traveled road along the north side. Largely closed but clad in aluminum, the north side contrasts with the southern exposure, which has more glazing, as well as a two-story triangular extension. Aligned with the parapet of a listed Victorian pub to the east, the building also pays homage to its surroundings with horizontal lines in the cladding that correspond to the window levels of the older neighboring building. At 6,490 square feet (603 square meters), the interior is large by the standards of new houses in London. The floors were conceptualized to reflect their purposes. These levels are designed as nearly independent parallel volumes whose configuration is not readily apparent when seen from the exterior. In fact, the house reveals little of its actual purpose from the outside—it stands as a smooth and silvery presence in a city that is more accustomed to stone in its residential areas. A feeling of enclosed space, or perhaps a perimeter of protection, is announced by a screened forecourt at ground level. This element of the design of the house is continued inside, but it gives way to complete openness on the upper level. The architect explains that as a result of "the sense of enclosure in the guest and music rooms compared with the expansive privacy of the master bedroom, the loose formality of the living space, and the open vistas of the roof terrace, the house offers a wide range of locations for different activities and states of mind. In this context, the staircases are designed to promote choice and continuity within a range of scenarios."

The architect masters transitions in materials and colors. The thin, elegant stairway bisects the space and emphasizes its generous height.

Both interior and exterior surfaces express a palette of textures and degrees of opacity and reflection of light.

2

House in Monterrey

Architects **Tadao Ando**
Location **Monterrey, Mexico** Year **2011**

This house was built on a 2.67-acre (1.08-hectare) site at the edge of a mountainous national park area. The residence overlooks the Roberto Garza Sada Center for Arts, Architecture, and Design of the University of Monterrey (completed in 2012), another project by Tadao Ando, built at the behest of the grandmother of the young client who commissioned this house. Ando explains, "The client requested a house that merges into the surrounding environment, bringing the beautiful views inside with perfect privacy. I conceived the house to realize this theme—open, but closed to the outside, but using geometry corresponding to the theme." The geometry consists in large part of a square that is topped by a Z-shaped volume. At no less than 16,350 square feet (1,519 square meters), this is by any measure a very large house. The architect explains, "This is a building of a size comparable to that of a small urban museum. Indeed, oftentimes the clients of such grand houses are also collectors of contemporary art, so it is not unusual for portions of their residences to be designed as galleries. What such clients seek are not buildings that contain conventional living spaces, but something with a greater public character." Exposed concrete, limestone, and granite are the main materials visible on both the interior and exterior of the structure. Ando states, "The private living zone is positioned on the lowest level around two triangular courtyards formed by the building's volumes. The public area, which contains a gallery, unravels into the Z-shaped volume that climbs the hillside across the two upper levels. The core of the house, the library, is contained by a wing that is angled against the building's main axis at 45 degrees to connect the private and public areas." Although bright colors are not part of the scheme, the Japanese architect says that in this house in Monterrey, he sought to "pay his highest respects to the Mexican architect Luis Barragán." Though Ando's work has a tendency to seem cold in photographs, his mastery of light and architectural volume, coupled in this case with spectacular views, brings real life to the house.

A bookcase (left) covers almost an entire wall. Concrete, usually associated with heaviness, becomes light in the hands of the Japanese master.

Ando's measured proportions and careful control of materials form a willful contrast with the natural environment, and yet the house profits fully from the beauty of its surroundings.

OVERLEAF Lit at night, the house seems like a haven of calm and beauty (left). The structured order of Ando's design, relying as usual entirely on geometric forms, encounters the irregular register of nature (right).

Allianz

3

I Tulipani House

Architects **Arkpabi**
Location **Cremona, Italy** Year **2009**

Designed by Cremona architects Arkpabi (Giorgio Palù and Michele Bianchi), this suspended house for an artist has a floor area of 2,368 square feet (220 square meters), plus an equivalent hanging garden space. Black, blue, and red volumes are perched on an older building. The architects state, "The purpose is to dematerialize the project, compacting the architecture, [while] maintaining the sequence of the inventions of the architectural composition. Even the interiors in the suspended villa obey this logic, introducing ambivalent geometries and transparency." Glass walls make the corners of the building "dematerialize," just as interior stairs with glass steps become nearly invisible and are contrasted with opaque and reflective walls. The ceilings are clad in maple, and works of art are scattered throughout the residence. The goal is to create intangible or fluid spaces. Other materials include grayed oak flooring and a wall covered in black leather. An elevator with one glass wall allows views into the house and opens into a glass cube in the roof garden. Motorized curtains are hidden in false ceilings. Transparency and immateriality characterize the interior, while unexpected combinations of color and form mark the exterior. The spatial and material surprises rendered in this project intimately connect the forms of the exterior to the unusual interior. The architects, both born in Cremona in 1964 and both educated at the Polytechnic University of Milan (from which they graduated in 1990), have designed a number of other residences and larger buildings in Cremona.

In contrast to the more traditional architectural environment in the background, the house breathes modern transparency, carried here even to a suspended Plexiglas chair.

The architects play on color and materials with the large blue glass cantilevered volume (left) opening onto a generous terrace. Inside, light, transparency, and opacity are put into an intriguing juxtaposition (right).

4

Zafra-Uceda House

Architects **No.MAD Arquitectos**
Location **Aranjuez, Spain** Year **2009**

An unusual aspect of the interiors of this house is that, at the request of the clients, there are no doors, but each area of the residence does have an established function. The surroundings of the house, essentially a golf course, are deemed "empty" and a "manmade environment of dubious quality" by the architect, Eduardo Arroyo. He employed various devices to combat this issue, such as a metal mesh façade that shields the sleeping and dining areas on the south not only from sun, but also from golf balls. While a concrete wall blocks out neighbors to the east, inside, according to the architect, an "iridescent polycarbonate wall changes colors with the light and runs parallel to a reflecting mirroring wall that multiplies the interior spaces." Expanding the interior space, Arroyo created a double-height living room with "panoramic perforations." Two terraces with a cactus garden that are enclosed on the sides but open to the sky are situated on the upper level, while the southern terrace frames distant views. Born in 1964 in Bilbao and educated at the prestigious Superior Technical School of Architecture of Madrid (from which he graduated in 1988), Arroyo is known for his inventive work, but also for taking sometimes unexpected positions in his statements. Thus, speaking of this 2,961-square-foot (250-square-meter) residence, which indeed does not exude an air of indulgence, he explains, "To the north, pieces of green marble, cut out with invisible lines, send a public message reminding us that the time for luxurious buildings has probably passed." Mostly in tones of gray and white, with a somewhat hard-edged appearance, the interiors are brightened not only by ample natural light, but also by sparse yet often colorful furnishings.

gular openings and volumes, together
th a play on materials such as wood,
ass, and metal, animate the architecture
d strengthen its rapport with the site.

Inside, furnishings and surfaces rival the simplicity of the architecture itself, but also introduce notes of color or contrasts between opacity and transparency.

5

Villa Vista

Architects **Shigeru Ban**
Location **Weligama, Sri Lanka** Year **2010**

Born in 1957, Shigeru Ban has earned an international reputation in the past few years with works such as his Centre Pompidou-Metz (2010) and the Pritzker Architecture Prize that he was awarded in 2014. He has designed many private residences, but perhaps none quite so large as this villa, which is 8,880 square feet (825 square meters). The client, Koenraad Pringiers, contacted the architect after seeing the relief work he did in Sri Lanka after the 2004 tsunami (Tsunami Reconstruction Project, Kirinda, Sri Lanka, 2007). The house sits on a hilltop overlooking the Indian Ocean in the southern resort town of Weligama. The interiors are closely related to the exteriors and were designed to highlight three different framed views selected by the architect. "The first," says Ban, "is the view of the ocean seen from the jungle in the valley, framed perpendicularly by the external corridor from the existing house to this house and the roof. The next is the horizontal view of the ocean from the hilltop framed by a large roof supported by poles with a 22-meter span and the floor. The last is the view of the cliff, which glows red at sunset; this is viewed through a square frame composed of 4 meters of solid wood in the main bedroom." Ban placed an emphasis on such locally produced materials as teak, cement boards, and woven coconut leaves. The design is marked by a number of open slat walls with adjustable shutters that let in natural light and cast a variety of shadows. Traditional walls and stairs were eschewed in favor of horizontally stacked, open platforms, and furnishings have been kept to a minimum.

is tropical climate, Shigeru Ban
actively on the very open design to
interior and exterior blend together.
ngs carefully frame views.

THE WELIGAMA BAY

An undulating ceiling and windows that admit light at determined points enliven this view of the interior space, which gives an indication of the vast area in this residence.

At the entrance, a horizontally laid wood wall contrasts with the white surfaces of the overhanging roof and exterior walls of the house.

Laguna Beach is located in southern Orange County on the Pacific coast. Set on a half-acre (2,023-square-meter) plot of land, the McElroy Residence offers spectacular ocean views. The entryway is bordered by a 50-foot (15.24-meter) teak-covered wall. Although local regulations allowed an overall height of no more than 11 feet (3.35 meters), the architects succeeded in giving the living spaces a generous feeling by designing oversize sliding glass doors that disappear when they are open. The result is an almost seamless transition between indoors and out, especially fitting given the mild climate of Laguna Beach. A broad horizontal roof is supported by stone and wood walls as well as thin steel columns. The architects explain, "Guest and children's bedrooms open onto the protected courtyard in the rear, while the master suite commands a layered view of the swimming pool and the ocean. The master bath opens onto its own private meditation garden nestled between the house and the land behind it. The stone floor extends to the outside, where it is joined by areas delineated with teak, concrete, and landscaping to provide a variety of outdoor entertaining and living areas perfect for enjoying warm weather." In fact the 7,800-square-foot (725-square-meter) house revolves around an open-air courtyard. A basement level contains the garage, a fitness room, and storage and service spaces. Flooring is marble, limestone, and onyx, and a number of different patterned fabrics appear as well. Takashi Yanai, head of the firm's residential arm, states, "To tie the house to its location, I chose components that represent earth and water, and I kept the pieces low and understated to preserve sight lines and the sense of openness." Born in New York in 1946 and based in Culver City, California, Steven Ehrlich studied at Rensselaer Polytechnic Institute in Troy, New York (graduating in 1969), before exploring indigenous vernacular architecture in North and West Africa from 1969 to 1977. He opened his own firm in 1979 and, in addition to numerous houses in California, he has completed projects in several other countries. Yanai joined the firm in 1999 and became a principal in 2007.

Full-height openings enable the kitchen (inside) and the pool (outside) to form a contiguous space that is usable for much of the year.

The California climate allows for many spaces in the house that are at once sheltered and private, but still outdoors.

Full-height glazing can be retracted into the walls, leaving living areas such as this one completely open on the sides.

7

Villa Vallarta

Architects **Ezequiel Farca Architecture and Design**
Location **Puerto Vallarta, Mexico** Year **2013**

This residence is located on the marina in the Pacific Ocean resort town of Puerto Vallarta. The main materials used are oak carpentry, pietra serena, Biarritz statuario, and Carrara marble for floors, and a precast concrete façade made with custom molds that mimic the texture of wood. These panels were also employed in some interior spaces. Ezequiel Farca was inspired by California beach houses with their combination of contemporary architecture and 1950s style. The public areas of the house are on the ground level, with the private spaces above. The residence includes a fitness center, a home theater, two Jacuzzis, a terrace with a swimming pool, a fire pit, and eight bedrooms. The total floor area is a very generous 36,597 square feet (3,400 square meters) on a site that measures a bit over 1.5 acres (6,184 square meters). Each room has floor-to-ceiling windows that open onto private terraces. The living/dining space is surrounded by glass curtain walls that open onto the terrace and pool area. The architect explains, "Furniture and decorative elements were chosen and designed specifically for the project. Colors and linen fabrics bring warmth and a relaxing ambiance to the beach house, while custom walnut furniture adds a touch of the elegance of the 1950s, emphasized by vintage decoration elements chosen for the house." Green walls and roofs insulate the house and reduce the need to use air-conditioning. The main focus of the architectural design was to create an open connection between the interior and the exterior with its views of the ocean. This was done while preserving the privacy of the bedrooms and other nonpublic areas.

The entrance sequence plays on horizontal lines formed not only by the steps but also by the overhanging canopy and the striated precast-concrete walls.

A sunken outdoor seating area around a hearth, an overhanging terrace, and a sensational view make the indoor-outdoor style of the house.

8

AA House

Architects **OAB**
Location **Sant Cugat del Vallès, Spain** Year **2009**

Set near a golf course in the Vallès Occidental area near Barcelona, this structure has an orthogonal layout and was compared by the architect, Carlos Ferrater, to a "boat anchored in a green sea of grass." This metaphor extends to the four narrow staircases that are hidden "like those on a boat." Service facilities are concealed below the living spaces, while a lower-level garage houses a collection of cars. Above the main space, the client's map collection is kept in a loft that can be reached via a folding ladder in the library. The kitchen, the focus of much attention, is described as "a world opening completely onto the garden and bathed in natural daylight, a systematic laboratory of nutrition, care, cleaning, and work." According to the architect, "This is a house that is contrary to itself: telluric and anchored at the base, and yet light and floating like a balloon about to leave the ground. It takes us back to the idea of a 'house' as an authentic archetype, as understood by Gaston Bachelard and Luis Barragán, with a basement and an attic. This house, rich in intensity and meaning, contains a multitude of symbols. It is a house on a lovely piece of land, all garden, that floats above the grass." Other architectural references include houses by Louis I. Kahn, Alison and Peter Smithson, and Ray and Charles Eames. The design is based on a 23-foot-square (7-meter-square) orthogonal network on which 45-degree diagonals are "overlaid as in a musical staff, which serves as a base for the composition of the project." Large by any standard, the house is 12,917 square feet (1,200 square meters). Based in Barcelona, Ferrater was born in 1944. He founded his current firm, OAB, in 2006 with Xavier Martí—with whom he designed this house—Lucía Ferrater, Borja Ferrater, and project director Núria Ayala.

Angled white walls, enlivened here by a bookshelf, are contrasted with the wooden floor. Furnishings and decoration are minimal, in keeping with the space itself.

Spatial surprises are part of the interest of the house—as, for example, in the white stairway (left) that slices through space to the lower level.

An indoor pool (right) lies between a metal mesh ceiling and wooden surfaces. The broad glazed wall can be opened.

Tomás Alcoverro EL DECANO
Maragall

With few if any paintings or other items on the walls, books take on a central role, here enveloping a desk with a generous view of the garden.

9

House K

Architects **Sou Fujimoto**
Location **Nishinomiya, Japan** Year **2012**

This relatively small 1,270-square-foot (118-square-meter) residence showcases the architectural inventiveness of Sou Fujimoto, who was born in 1971. He established his firm, Sou Fujimoto Architects, in Tokyo in 2000. This house is located in Nishinomiya, a residential area in Hyogo prefecture between the densely populated cities of Kobe and Osaka. On a site with a view of a wooded area to the west, the architect created a diagonal rooftop garden. The architect's concept was that "the garden and the interior be richly contiguous." The interior has three different levels, each of which provides access to a roof garden. A semi-basement level with living space is excavated about 5 feet (1.5 meters) into the ground. Dining and kitchen spaces are near the entrance at ground level, and a nursery/living room is up steps about 8 feet (2.5 meters) higher. The master bedroom and bathroom are located beneath the steps. The emphasis on free movement from the roof garden to the interior and the layered interior spaces create a dynamic set of spatial relationships. "You can move freely in and out that way," says Fujimoto. "I wanted to generate a more natural geographic relationship between inside and outside different from standard architecture, where the garden and floor levels are distinct from each other." Other well-known Japanese architects, such as Toyo Ito, have actively speculated about the relationship between nature and architecture, creating purposely artificial representations of nature. Here, potted plants that might be interpreted differently in other parts of the world bring a natural presence to a house whose configuration evokes a hill or a mountain. The wind and sun, common manifestations of nature in Japan, are also present in this unusual house.

The architect is a master of intermediate spaces with indeterminate functions such as this raised platform with a large window.

The interior of the house is largely open, with the different levels reached by open stairways, or even a ladder leading to the rooftop garden.

10

Edward Street House

Architects **Sean Godsell Architects**
Location **Melbourne, Australia** Year **2011**

This house is located about two and a half miles (four kilometers) from the business district of Melbourne in an "inner suburban" area described by the architect, Sean Godsell, as "a tough part of town." It was designed for an artist and a musician and their three children. The house has an area of 2,583 square feet (240 square meters). In describing his own thoughts on the process of designing this house, Godsell says, "Public and private realms are defined via these investigations rather than consciously considered, and cultural overlaps between the traditional Japanese house and the traditional colonial house in the Australian context are a constant source of inspiration." Aside from these cultural sources of inspiration, the house design takes into account the grittiness of the neighborhood, by showing only a "tough, almost impenetrable steel hide." This galvanized steel shell also serves as a sunscreen and wraps upward to form a roof garden. Godsell continues, "To offset this strategy, the interior needed to be as warm and nurturing as possible and so wood is the dominant material—oiled and recycled blackbutt for the floor with blackbutt-faced plywood on the walls and ceilings. All the spaces in the house are divided by large sliding plywood panels and built-in furniture—daybeds, desks, and bookshelves all adopt the same materiality. The cocoonlike quality of the interior provides a comforting contrast to the harsh urban environment beyond." Godsell, born in Melbourne in 1960, specializes in houses in natural environments and before this project he had not designed an urban residence since 1997. In this instance, the contrast between the armorlike exterior and the "cozy" wooden interiors can be seen as an innovative response to a rather difficult urban site. Godsell refers to traditional Japanese houses in his analysis of the public/private dichotomy. Whereas modern Japanese urban houses often have exteriors that appear closed, their interiors can look cold to outside observers. Godsell's approach to this issue was to seek interior warmth by designing a protective nest.

Recycled and oiled blackbutt plywood covers the walls and ceilings, giving an enclosed feeling of warmth to the interiors.

Natural light enters the house in a filtered manner, but the overall impression is one of closed spaces with warm wood surfaces and metal finishings.

11
Pilotis in a Forest

Architects **Go Hasegawa**
Location **Kita-Karuizawa, Japan** Year **2010**

With just 829 square feet (77 square meters) of usable floor space, the interior of this weekend house in the Gunma prefecture is described by the architect as “compact.” The house stands high off the ground in a forest and forms a covered patio for barbecues and other events. This house can be said to challenge the very concept of the interior (and exterior) of a house. Go Hasegawa states, “Doing my best to leave the trees undisturbed, I decided to create a group of pilotis in the forest. By making them tall enough so that even when you are in the bottom section of the house, you can see the trunks of the tall trees, I used the forest as the building’s walls. By placing a large bench and table outside and hanging a hammock between the trees, I’ve made it so that everyone can relax in the forest. In contrast, I created an aerial living room in the small attic-like space with 6-foot [1.75-meter] high beams at the lowest point. By making the scale of the room one size smaller than normal and creating a lower than normal dining table and chairs, I attempted to convey the sense that the natural environment outside is larger and closer.” The issue, of course, is not only the relationship between inside and outside, but also the interface between natural and built environments—an issue of particular importance to Japanese architects, who are often confronted by densely built urban sites. That is not the case here, and Hasegawa has drawn on images and thoughts that go back to the very origins of architecture. Like a treehouse, the residence plays on both the idea of protection from the elements and acceptance of the natural environment. In nearly every sense, this house was designed at the edge of architectural space. Interior and exterior give way to each other continually, while the natural and the artificial also act together to define space in an innovative manner.

Wooden interiors offer generous views of the forest environment, creating a kind of symbiosis between the architecture and the surrounding trees.

A suspended stairway (left) leads from the forest floor up to the suspended living area of the house. Interior spaces (right) are finished in wood, but openings such as the one seen here allow views of the forest, beyond and below.

The light-colored wood, specially designed table and cabinetry, and ample glass surfaces give an impression of enveloping lightness.

Tsai Residence and Guesthouse

Architects **HHF + Ai Weiwei**
Location **Ancram, New York** Year **2008/2011**

HHF architects was founded in 2003 in Basel, Switzerland by Tilo Herlach, Simon Hartmann, and Simon Frommenwiler. They have worked often with the Chinese artist Ai Weiwei, as was the case for these projects located in Ancram, in Columbia County, New York. They first completed the 4,036-square-foot (375-square-meter) residence of Christopher Tsai and André Stockamp in 2008. The composition is made up of four connected volumes that were built in wood and clad in corrugated metal on the outside and gypsum panels inside. Intended for the exhibition of works of art such as the collectors' pieces by Ai Weiwei, the interiors have ample natural light that is brought in through openings in the metal shells. *The New York Times* wrote in 2008 that the house is elegant and slightly forbidding on the outside but expansive and light-filled on the inside. The architects explain, "The living room focuses on the different light conditions needed for an existing and future art collection, while the great view into the nearby countryside is present without being dominant." The second project carried out for these clients on the same site by HHF and Ai Weiwei was their 2011 Guesthouse, a 2,357-square-foot (219-square-meter) timber structure covered with corrugated Cor-ten steel. It includes a work area and art gallery as well as a bedroom in a Y-shaped plan. The lower level, occupying almost half the overall floor area, contains a garage. Most of the interior walls, ceilings, and floors are clad in wood. The architects state, "The relationship of the Tsai residence to the guesthouse reflects HHF's philosophy, namely to use what already exists at a site as a source of inspiration."

Elegant volumes and contrasts in materials mark the space. Natural light is admitted not only through the full-height glazed doors but also from above.

Interior spaces are simple and elegant, with relatively sparse furnishings and important works of contemporary art. These include pieces by the Chinese artist Ai Weiwei, a frequent partner of the architects in their projects.

13

Daeyang House

Architects **Steven Holl**
Location **Seoul, Korea** Year **2012**

Like much of the work of Steven Holl, this gallery/house, located in the Gangbuk area of Seoul, seeks to experiment with new areas in architectural design. It challenges the relationship of one volume to another and explores their interconnection with a water-filled basin. The architects explain, "The project was designed as an experiment parallel to a research studio on the architectonics of music. The basic geometry of the building is inspired by a 1967 sketch for a music score by the composer István Anhalt, 'Symphony of Modules,' which was discovered in a book by John Cage titled *Notations*." These references may not exactly clarify the nature of the design for most readers or viewers; in simpler terms, the complex is made up of three pavilions, one of which is devoted to the entrance, another that serves as an event space, and a third that is the home. No fewer than fifty-five skylight strips in the roofs animate the space with light during the day, while the surrounding water is essential to the spatial innovation of the architecture. Strips of glass in the reflecting pool also bring moving light into the lower-level white plaster and white granite gallery. The architects explain, "A visitor arrives through a bamboo garden wall at the entry court after opening the front door and ascending a low staircase. He or she can turn to see the central pond at eye level and take in all three pavilions, floating on their own reflections. The interiors of the pavilions are red and charcoal-stained wood with the skylights cutting through the wood ceilings." The interior of the 10,703-square-foot (994-square-meter) complex is of note because equal attention was paid to residential and gallery spaces. The two are integrated, while each also preserves its own individual character.

otographed empty of furnishings, the
use nonetheless expresses the mastery
space and light that is typical of
e architect.

The positioning of the basins, glass walls, and stairways creates a spatial ambiguity that permeates the project (left). Light comes from unexpected places, and materials succeed each other in an ordered play on reflections and opacity (right).

14

YTL Residence

Architects **Jouin Manku**
Location **Kuala Lumpur, Malaysia** Year **2008**

This astonishing house is the work of noted French designer Patrick Jouin and the architect Sanjit Manku, who were selected because the clients, members of a prominent Chinese-Malaysian family, liked Jouin's work for the Alain Ducasse restaurant at the Plaza Athénée in Paris. Sitting on a hilltop that looks toward the skyline of Kuala Lumpur, the residence was designed by two young creative minds who had never before built a house, yet its symbiotic relation to nature and its striking modernity make it a true standout. Jouin, who was responsible for the interior design of the house and developed the architectural concept with Manku, states, "For this project we were searching for a spatial and formal language as dramatic as the landscape itself—to create a home that is not a village house, nor a 'traditional tropical house,' yet at the same time was truly based on and almost at times mimicked the particular spatial character of the natural environment. We wished to create a project that would rest with ease among the dense tropical fauna." The house is divided into three areas—the family residence, public space in the base, and a guest area in a ring-shaped form at ground level. With its high ceilings and cantilevered lightness, the main level opens almost entirely to the exterior with sliding glass panels that are 13 feet (4 meters) high and nearly an inch (25 millimeters) thick. Although the house is fully air-conditioned, it breathes the humid air of Kuala Lumpur when its windows are open, which is usually the case, even when it is raining outside. Two spiral staircases designed by Jouin and Manku slice through the interior. One steel staircase recalls the spirals of Oscar Niemeyer, and the other resembles a great teak skeleton. Jouin explains, "The main spiral staircase brings lightness to the house, but we also wanted to design a sensual form. There is an organic aspect visible in the teak stairway. This is not a biomorphic house. It is not soft; it has strong elements that structure the space." Other interior features include an almost 20-foot- (6-meter-) long gray Carrara marble.

A massive block of marble selected by the architects forms the kitchen counter. The sloping wooden roof opens to a swimming pool and an expansive view of Kuala Lumpur.

PREVIOUS SPREAD The main living space features furnishings and a unique spiral staircase designed by the architects. The main bedrooms are on the upper level.

LEFT A downstairs reception area is used by the owners to greet guests, sometimes numbering hundreds at a time.

15

L House

Architects **Mathias Klotz and Edgardo Minond**
Location **Buenos Aires, Argentina** Year **2012**

This house seeks to occupy its site in Olivos, a residential neighborhood in Buenos Aires, to the fullest extent allowed by local regulations. The 79-by-177-foot (24-by-54-meter) site is rectangular, and every effort was made to incorporate existing trees and garden space. The architects make a point of saying that the exterior open spaces do not consist simply of leftover space, but are a real part of the design. The intention of Mathias Klotz in this instance was to "form a whole without boundaries between architecture and landscape." Generous glazing and openings create a real feeling of interaction between inside and outside. The materials used—concrete, steel, wood, and travertine marble for the floors—were selected by the architects and the client working in concert. The house has three bedrooms—one of which also serves as a playroom—a living room, a kitchen, and a service area. The master bedroom is on the upper floor. A pond in front of the house reflects the structure's concrete. Three concrete steps clad in travertine are cantilevered over the pond and lead to the house. Other ponds with aquatic plants and fish are situated around the house. An upper-floor terrace has a travertine floor accompanied by dry stones and creeping plants. The architects further explain that they sought "duality between light and heavy in terms of materiality." Reinforced-concrete walls do not touch the floor in the entrance or dining area access spaces. Steps anchored in the central supporting wall seem to float, while skylights along the walls bring in natural light from above. The 4,305-square-foot (400-square-meter) built area is augmented by 1,120 square feet (104 square meters) of semi-covered space.

Bare-faced concrete is used, but ceiling openings bring in natural light. Furnishings occupy and warm this space, which might otherwise remain quite cold.

A cantilevered portion of the house (left) creates a covered outside terrace. Though concrete generally seems heavy, here the overhanging volume seems to float in space. Inside, a suspended fireplace and full-height glazing bring in the natural setting and warmth (right).

In areas such as the kitchen and dining space (left) or the glazed corridor (right), the use of wood and outdoor greenery alleviates the significant presence of concrete, making the house convivial ard warm.

16

Twin Houses

Architects **Lussi+Halter Architekten**
Location **Kastanienbaum, Switzerland** Year **2011**

Designed by architects based in Lucerne, Switzerland, this 5,479-square-foot (509-square-meter) structure consists of two houses lodged in a single poured-in-place concrete cube that was essentially split down the middle. The house is divided in this way because architect Remo Halter had a plan to build his own house but did not have the means to take on the entire project. Another couple joined Halter and his wife. For the project, Halter and his partner at the time, Thomas Lussi, consciously referenced Le Corbusier's work (including the architect's Museum of Ahmedabad, 1957, and his Shodan House, 1956). Ramps leading up and down from the living area recall such works by Le Corbusier as the Villa Savoye (1931). A pool and terrace on the roof are shared by the two couples who own the houses. Further living and service areas, including housing for a geothermal heat pump system, are on the basement level. The use of concrete and triple glazing gives the house a very low energy profile. Set in a forested site, the residence features a glass façade at ground level, but black structural concrete was mainly used to build ceilings and walls, while Brazilian jatoba wood was employed on the floors and lower faces of the balconies. Balconies and terraces play a significant role in the design, connecting interior to exterior, or, as is the case in the master bedroom, serving to frame a view of the natural setting. Covered walkways and pine louvers provide both exposure to the outside and protection from the elements. The very basic cubic form of the houses and the use of black concrete give the whole a somewhat monumental, even mysterious air that makes it stand out in a part of Switzerland where more traditional residential buildings are much more common. Halter says, "Timeless architecture reaching beyond any momentary trends or unnecessary gimmicky shapes and forms—these are the aspirations we had in mind when conceiving the houses."

The rooftop terrace and pool combine an elevated basin with a wooden deck, the whole conceived in a well-designed manner.

Dark wood and metal harmonize with concrete to form interiors that have a cave-like atmosphere within the green setting visible through full-height glazing.

SAO
PAULO

agustín hernández

17

Ma House

Architects **MADA s.p.a.m.**
Location **Pasadena, California** Year **2011**

Ma Qingyun studied architecture in his native China before obtaining his master of architecture degree from the University of Pennsylvania in 1991. He established his firm, MADA s.p.a.m. (which stands for strategy, planning, architecture, and media), in Shanghai in 1995. He has been the dean of the School of Architecture at the University of Southern California since 2006. For his own residence in Pasadena, he conceived an addition to a "mid-century Californian entertaining home." The three-story "semi-public" addition includes living space, an office, and a gallery. The wood-frame structure has a "deep purple, organic, and alien" shotcrete finish. The double-height gallery with adjoining private rooms bridges over the existing one-level entertainment space of the earlier house. A third-floor dance studio for the architect's wife, Shouning Li, that can be easily converted into a reception area is part of the new space. Circulation through the old and new spaces is via a "continuous circulatory loop." In contrast to the roughness of the exterior of the addition, "the interior space is clean, crisp, and smooth." The floor area of the addition is 3,660 square feet (340 square meters). The architect states, "MADA s.p.a.m. has defined itself by strategic negotiations that frequently result in challenging the political and social status quo. Such practices and character extend into the design of this single family home, transforming the process into one of precision engineering and of testing the boundaries of local codes. The Ma residence is the result of the intersection of careful analysis of the needs of the Ma family with the challenges of breaking free from the conventional mid-century Californian home. Through the use of a circular ramp, the old single-story house is seamlessly fused with the new three-story addition. The expansion allows for aggressive growth in program and function to meet the lifestyle needs of a family of four."

e new part of the residence,
windows add extra natural light
he architect describes as
smooth" space.

The juncture between old and new is handled with angled walls and the introduction of white surfaces into a formerly traditional interior environment.

OVERLEAF A long dining table is set up in the new space (left), with a rough rock wall apparent in the background. The old house meets the new annex (right).

18

Leaf House

Architects **Mareines + Patalano**
Location **Angra dos Reis, Brazil** Year **2008**

Located one hour's drive south of the city of Rio de Janeiro, this house was inspired by the Indian architecture of Brazil, according to the designers. The name of the residence derives from its large leaflike roof made with a laminated eucalyptus structure that protects the house and in-between spaces from the sun. The roof structure is covered with small Pinus taeda wood tiles. The architects state, "These in-between open spaces represent the essence of the design. They are the social areas, where the owner of the house and his guests spend most of their time. The very generous heights of these spaces, which vary from 10 to 30 feet (3 to 9 meters), allow the southeast trade winds from the ocean to pass through the building, providing natural ventilation and passive cooling to both the enclosed and the open spaces." They call this system "low-tech eco-efficiency." Through a central steel column the roof collects rainwater, which is used for the garden and toilets. An effort was made throughout not to separate manmade elements from nature, creating a fusion between interior and exterior. The house is built on a plot nearly 10 acres (4 hectares) in size. A curving swimming pool actually enters the house and passes below the dining room, where it becomes a pond with aquatic plants and fish. Indian-style hammocks are used on the veranda. An emphasis is placed on natural surface finishes—stones from the site were used for tiles, and recycled wood from old electrical posts was also employed, as was locally harvested wood from managed forests. Pre-oxidized copper cladding is seen in parts of the project, "relating to the prevailing green of the designed and natural landscape along with the organic composition of the house and rich diversity of textures and rhythms," according to Mareines + Patalano. The architects were also responsible for the interiors of the 8,611-square-foot (800-square-meter) house and even designed some of the furniture.

An angled deck and canopy lead to the beach and boat dock. This space is covered but, in keeping with Brazil's climate, it is broadly open to the exterior.

The treehouse-like atmosphere of the interior is inspired by traditional Brazilian architecture (left). The exteriors also adopt this mode, with carefully designed touches such as a lozenge-shaped wooden terrace (right).

Peter Marino / Architect
Lalanne(s)

19

Palm Beach Residence

Architects **Peter Marino**
Location **Palm Beach, Florida** Year **2010**

This rather large 8,000-square-foot (743-square-meter) house was built for a New York couple with an interest in Southeast Asian furniture and art, as well as contemporary paintings. The 1.5-acre (6,070 square meter) site faces the Atlantic Ocean and is located at the north end of Palm Beach. The design of the house takes into account the client's interest in South East Asia, as well as their collection of contemporary art, but the courtyard-style house also refers to its actual location, through the choice of materials such as pecky cypress wood and Florida coral stone, which is used on a fireplace wall. The owners' collection includes works by such artists as Damien Hirst, but also such objects as an eighteenth-century Goan table made of solid jacaranda wood. Works by designers such as Ingo Maurer lights or chairs by Philippe Hiquilly are complemented by such pieces as a bed by Romanian-born French designer Maria Pergay. A work was commissioned from the Paris-based installation artist Guy Limone for the powder room of the house. An Antelope Table by Claude and François-Xavier Lalanne, pieces by the American furniture artist Wendell Castle, the French ceramist Georges Jouve, and the French designer Yonel Lebovici are to be found in the company of Southeast Asian lintels or a Richard Prince cabinet. The house thus combines the exceptional design talents of Peter Marino with a collection of objects that fully reflect the personality of the owners of the house; it is a house just for them.

A painting by Richard Prince of a nurse and chairs designed by Wendell Castle reside in the library of the house.

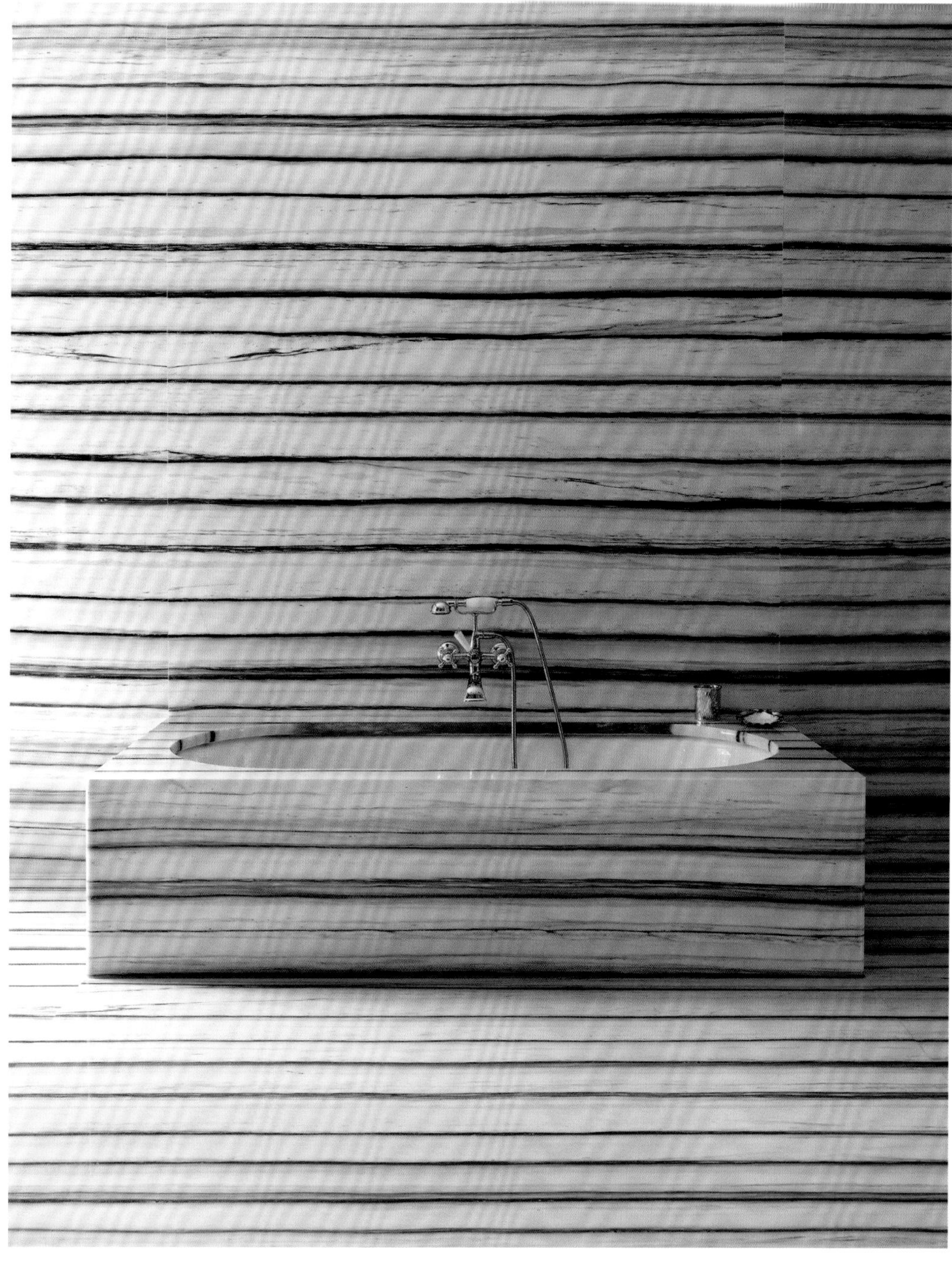

DALI
ROBERT DELAUNAY
YVES KLEIN
FRANK KUPKA
EL LISSITZKY

PREVIOUS SPREAD A Damien Hirst Butterfly painting shares the space with an Antelope Table by Claude and François-Xavier Lalanne (left). A bathtub blends in with the background wall (right).

LEFT A large painting by Richard Prince takes center stage in the living room of the Palm Beach house.

20

Fire Island House

Architects **Richard Meier**
Location **Fire Island, New York** Year **2013**

Set on the beach at Fair Harbor on Fire Island, this residence has a large, flat roof that overhangs a raised platform and two staggered volumes containing a double-height living room on one side and a media room and ground-floor kitchen with an upper-level master bedroom on the other side. Double-height curtain walls on three sides mark the oceanfront façades. The major materials employed in the structure are white-painted cedar, aluminum curtain walls, and wood flooring. The architects state, "The materials palette for the project was minimal and understated, with an emphasis on lightness and transparency: glass, wood, and white finishes reflect the natural colors and beauty of the surrounding bay." The house has a floor area of 2,000 square feet (186 square meters) plus 1,700 square feet (158 square meters) of deck space. The house is somewhat sparsely furnished. The owners had an earlier residence on Fire Island that burned down in 2011, taking their possessions and memorabilia with it. That left them open to a stark white interior, which is what architect Richard Meier, who takes an active interest in decoration as well as design, prefers. The house stands out from much more traditional wooden buildings nearby in more ways than one—it perches on wood piles driven 10 feet (3 meters) below sea level. A steel frame strong enough to support 25 tons of glass was built on top of the piles. The design inevitably had to take into account the possibility of strong storms, and in 2012 the as-yet-incomplete house survived Hurricane Sandy. Though deemed a "mini-skyscraper" locally, the house is small enough that it hasn't generated quite the same controversy that contemporary architecture has garnered in some places.

Within a space characterized by Richard Meier's signature white style and generous use of natural light, a stairway evokes ship design. Both the wood floor and the streaming daylight provide warmth.

21

Luxembourg House

Architects **Richard Meier**
Location **Luxembourg** Year **2012**

Built on a secluded, wooded site, this residence, constructed with metal panels, glass, stone, and wood flooring, has a total area of 10,500 square feet (975 square meters). The south and east sides of the house, which face neighbors and the street, are opaque to preserve privacy. Interior and exterior are in constant dialogue thanks to the use of large glazed surfaces and terraces. A circular spine cuts through the volumes of the house, dividing it into a solid zone on the south and a void zone on the north that has a lighter steel structure. The glass façade takes in both elements. The main public areas of the house are on the ground level, including an open kitchen, a guest room, and a playroom on the south and double-height living and dining areas on the north. Bedrooms and a master suite are on the southern part of the upper floor, as are a study, library, and lounge. Although Richard Meier is well known for his signature white designs and geometric vocabulary, he proves here again that these defining elements leave a great deal of room for invention and variety. A good part of this variety is provided by the ever-changing natural light that suffuses his architecture in general and this residence in particular. Aside from passive energy strategies having to do with thermal mass, orientation, and maximization of natural light, the house also has a controlled heat recovery ventilation system, radiant floor heating, a green roof, and rainwater recycling. A geothermal ground source heat pump and heat exchanger are also part of the overall energy conservation scheme.

Meier, as always, plays on white forms and generous glazing. The dark floor provides a contrast of tones, and the relatively sparse furnishings allow the architecture to give its full measure.

Meier's houses almost always feature double-height living spaces and full glazing. Fireplaces add to the warmth already suggested by the wooden floors on the upper level (left). Successive staircases seem to float in space (right).

22

Georgica Pond Residence

Architects **Shelton, Mindel & Associates**
Location **East Hampton, New York** Year **2007**

For this project, the designers were faced with the specific problem of renovating a modernist wooden house dating from the late 1970s without changing its footprint or removing any exterior walls or windows. The house had curving walls with vertical siding and some floor-to-ceiling glazing. The interior plan of the house was opened up, creating a double-height glazed living space situated where the two wings of the 5,500-square foot (511-square-meter) residence come together. Interior walls, clad in cedar that had darkened with age, were sanded, and terra-cotta tiling on the floors was reconditioned. A 25-foot (7.5-meter) round gray rug was used to neutralize the earth-toned color and textures of the living space. The designers explain, “In order to respect the sculptural forms of the walls, large-scale groups of furniture float freely and become architectural elements themselves in scale with the larger whole. Two very long overscale sofas give the tall living room a low horizon—and open their arms like a compass to the view of the water beyond.” The house is made up of two wings that come together in the central living area. The late Peter Shelton stated, “We tried to accept the building and embrace what it had to offer. The question was how to honor the old while bringing it forward.” Taking more liberty with the interiors than with the outside forms of the house, the designers reconfigured the master bedroom area, as well as the guest rooms and kitchen. The goal was to “seamlessly integrate architecture and interior design,” a challenging task given the origins of the house, but one that was well accomplished.

A tile floor and walls of wood or stone are featured in the double-height living area. Every detail of the architecture and furnishings is in a refined style.

Curving wooden walls (left) create a degree of privacy while also enlivening the space. In the large living area (right) wooden walls and tile floors are bathed in natural light, which comes primarily from the high, band windows.

23

Waterside Pool House

Architects **Shelton, Mindel & Associates**
Location **Long Island, New York** Year **2007**

A combination of designer furniture and very high glazed walls makes the relationship between the pool house and the outdoors transparent and inviting.

The designers were asked to make use of a garage and mechanical building to create a pool house and residential space with a bedroom, kitchen, bath, and outdoor area. The project also integrates the property's swimming pool and sculpture garden. Peter Shelton and Lee Mindel created a double-height area on the pool side of the building. On the street side, the structure matches adjacent buildings in appearance and height so that the "opaque, seemingly traditional building type turns the corner into a modernist two-story, light-filled cube." Interior and exterior are integrated by using Bauhaus-style building blocks as indoor and outdoor furniture. A concrete floor finish relates in color to the stone and wood employed outside. Playing on texture and color, a concrete-colored rug is used in the seating area of the living space. Lighting comes from porthole windows and orange plastic wall lights by Verner Panton.

The designers selected a round Poul Kjaerholm dining table and marine blue porpoise-shaped cantilevered Luigi Colani chaises longues that serve as interior sculptures. The bedroom, bathroom, stairway, and storage areas were made with maple, and upstairs furnishings are in wood, wicker, and linen. The designers state, "The upstairs bedroom becomes a maple tree house that faces the view of the sculpture garden, swimming pool, outdoor room, and creek." Interest is generated by the intentional juxtaposition of an apparently rather "normal" street-side structure with the clarity and modern design of the interiors, particularly in the living space and its transition to the exterior around the pool. The upstairs, on the other hand, is treated in a mix of textures and colors, making it inviting and modern, at once in harmony with the rest of the house yet different.

The pool house (left) stands out not only because of its geometric simplicity but also because of details such as the external stairway. The bedroom (right) is more enclosed and intimate.

24

Cloudline

Architects **Toshiko Mori**
Location **Columbia County, New York** Year **2011**

Located on a cliff above the Hudson River Valley in Columbia County, New York, this 6,200-square-foot (576-square-meter) residence is intended to "maximize its relation to the landscape." The house faces a wooded area to the rear and the eastern side is partially below grade, while the western exposure is generously glazed to allow views that extend for up to 50 miles (80 kilometers). The house was intentionally designed to play on the juxtaposition of views of the natural setting and contemporary art. Designed for the English-born New York art dealer Sean Kelly and his wife, Mary, the house is filled with works of art by the likes of Marina Abramovic, Antony Gormley, Jannis Kounellis, Juan Muñoz, Ian Hamilton Finlay, and Joseph Kosuth, some of which were created specifically for the house. An open-plan lower level contains the living, dining, and kitchen spaces. A library/archive "anchors the center circulation space," while bedrooms are placed at the perimeter of the upper level, offering both views and ample natural light. The relatively small openings in the upper part of the house purposefully contrast with the fully glazed lower level. Overhangs on the south and west façades reduce solar gain, while photovoltaic panels on the roof provide energy to heat water for the house. Plain concrete floors can be seen as a reference to similar floors in the contemporary art galleries of New York. As it happens, Toshiko Mori was also the architect behind Sean Kelly's new gallery, located at 475 Tenth Avenue in New York. The gallery project won a 2013 AIA New York Chapter Design Award for interiors.

Toshiko Mori's design is subtle, here opening this relatively modest living space almost entirely to the natural views and light.

In both the sequence of living spaces (left) and the staircase (right)—with its overhead lighting, integrated handrail, and work of art—the architect demonstrates a sophistication that speaks of the multiple possibilities of modern architecture.

The upper level of the house appears to be more weighty than the largely glazed ground floor. The downstairs spaces are much more open than the private second floor.

ULYSSES

Place
Parts
Whole
Context
Meaning

25

House in Connecticut II

Architects **Toshiko Mori**
Location **New Canaan, Connecticut** Year **2009**

The original house on this property, the Breuer House II, was designed by Marcel Breuer in 1951 for himself and his family. Between 1976 and 1982, it was extensively renovated by the architect Herbert Beckhard, an associate of Breuer's, who added a children's wing, a garage, a swimming pool, a pool house, and an attached guesthouse. Robert and Susan Bishop bought the house in 2005. They removed most of the additions designed by Beckhard and commissioned Toshiko Mori to renovate the original residence and to add a new freestanding structure. The plan included renovation of the original house and of the Beckhard pool house, for a total involved floor area of 7,000 square feet (650 square meters).

The original Breuer house measures 2,300 square feet (214 square meters) and contains the public spaces, including living room, dining room, family room, and kitchen, while the new addition contains the master bedroom suite, children's rooms, and utility spaces, including a garage. The addition is connected to the Breuer house via a connecting stair "enclosed in glass of varying transparency." Mori explains, "The original house, Breuer's personal home for twenty-five years, is small but possesses monumental stone walls. Our addition is taller and larger, and its base is the same height as the original house. The glass box topping our addition has a different translucency, opacity, and transparency, creating a mutable effect that diminished its size through the reflection of nature and light. The vertical extenuation from the taller and lighter addition contrasts with and increases the gravitas of the original house. It is a study in monumentality, size ,and scale." Mori has had other experience working on or near famous twentieth-century houses. In 2009, she completed the new visitor center for Frank Lloyd Wright's Darwin D. Martin House (1905) in Buffalo, New York. She also designed the 2005 renovation of the modernist John Black Lee's Lee House II in New Canaan (1956), and an addition to a 1957 Paul Rudolph house in Sarasota, Florida. Mori is currently the Robert P. Hubbard Professor in the Practice of Architecture at the Harvard Graduate School of Design and was chair of the department of architecture from 2002 to 2008. She is principal of Toshiko Mori Architect, which she established in 1981 in New York City.

The architect uses the cantilevered glass and steel upper level to create a sheltered terrace on the ground floor. The upper volume is completely transparent and seems almost weightless.

Interior volumes offer different heights and admit light through windows placed at several levels, including a skylight (left). An exterior view (right) shows the ample glazing and the angled design.

26

Walls in the Landscape

Architects **Susanne Nobis**
Location **Grossburgwedel, Germany** Year **2009**

This single-story residence includes an exhibition space for photography and other art forms. It is located just outside the town of Burgwedel, surrounded by open fields and an avenue lined with twenty pairs of old oak trees. The goal of the architect, Susanne Nobis, was to make the house, with its full-height glazed surfaces and Cor-ten steel walls, "intertwine fluently" with the landscape. More specifically, according to Nobis, the Cor-ten walls "make a colorful analogy with the old trees in the landscape." Though it is tempting to see this structure as a minimalist or simply modernist take on the single-story house, Nobis has given the stele-like Cor-ten walls a monumental presence in the green landscape, as though she also intended to create a piece of environmental or land art. The placement of the steel blocks runs beyond the strict outline of the house to form partially covered terraces. The transparency of the glass surfaces creates a striking contrast with the opaque steel walls; in photographs it looks as if the entire interior is open to the outside park environment. A narrow skylight over the rear wall brings indirect overhead natural light into the space. The architect states, "The inner workings of the house are enhanced by emerging variations in the light." The main entrance of the structure axis runs from north to south. Walls on both sides provide space for the art, with a large skylight offering further natural illumination for the work. Nobis was born in Munich in 1963. She studied architecture in Munich, London, and Berlin, then worked in the offices of Renzo Piano, Herzog + Partner, and Ackermann + Partner before eventually creating her own office in Munich.

Full-height glazing offers views of the natural environment and encloses rectilinear space with wooden floors and steel fittings.

MARC CHAGALL
EL LISSITZKY

The library space (left) is enclosed between two high glazed walls. Dark steel and wood floors create a protective shell with a white plaster roof. The furniture is largely black, inspired by the architecture. Cor-ten steel walls are used to finish the volumes (right).

27 Toward Landscape

Architects **Susanne Nobis**
Location **Berg, Germany** Year **2010**

The main materials of this 3,487-square-foot (324-square-meter) double house are spruce, aluminum, and glass. Two long structural timber shells recall the traditional boathouses seen on the shores of nearby Lake Starnberg, a rather chic residential area outside of Munich. Says the architect, Susanne Nobis, "Our aim was not to compete with nature and to preserve the view onto the lake, as well as the valuable vista into the countryside with its old tree population." The first half of the double house contains living, dining, and cooking spaces. Here, the entire wood-clad volume is open, with no partitions, while shelving gives a rhythm and visual richness to the side walls. In the second volume, there is a ground-floor office and an upper level with a bedroom, bathroom, and "installation room." The side walls of the house volumes are closed to maintain a sufficient degree of thermal insulation. Wooden terraces are situated at the end of the fully glazed lateral openings of the two volumes. A continuous skylight band brings natural light into the entire 57-foot (17.4-meter) length of the buildings. The living area volume was built with a glue binder construction technique, while the bedroom volume is a timber post-and-beam design with a thick wooden ceiling. A folded titanium-sheet shell encloses the rough timber exterior. According to Nobis, "The architectural concept is based upon an absolutely consistent appearance between the roof and the façade that blends into a single visual unit." The two volumes are connected by a simple glazed passageway.

The wooden shell of the house has a glazed slit at its uppermost level, with walls that are also completely glazed.

Zug um Zug

ZUG um ZUG
ABOUT TIME

DA VINCI
MARK ROTHKO
Francis Bacon

LANVIN

28

211 Elizabeth Street

Architects **Roman and Williams**
Location **New York, New York** Year **2009**

This seven-story new-build condominium structure with a hand-crafted brick façade is located in the Nolita area of Manhattan, at the corner of Prince Street. The first "ground-up" residential project designed by Roman and Williams, the building looks for all the world like an older structure and is quite at home in this largely historic neighborhood. "For us, better than being nostalgic, we are just carrying on a tradition that we like to think never ended," says firm principal Stephen Alesch. "It seems things took a detour for a long time into convenient construction and easy ways out. We see this as a continuation of, say, the period prior to the Great Depression, before beefy, strong, solid American architecture lost its way. All of our projects tend to be a bit pro-American in design and construction, which we believe holds great value." The 33,357-square-foot (3,098-square-meter) project included all interiors, as well as ground-level storefronts. Interiors of the fifteen one- and two-bedroom apartments feature contrasting Danish wood kitchens trimmed with high-gloss black paint. Roman and Williams paid careful attention to such elements as sight line in the interior design. "The grandeur of center lines and sight line give a little formality," states Alesch. "When you come out of your bedroom door and there is a sight line from your window to your living room or dining room, it makes you stand up a little straighter, be a little more upright. It's like putting on a jacket." The building lobby has black back-painted glass and trim, slate floors, a slate and walnut desk, and custom brass sconces. The project was the winner of the 2010 Palladio Award for excellence in traditional design.

Taking into account typical New York ceiling heights and volumes, the design as well as the furnishings here play on the black window frames and create an atmosphere that is warm but still modern.

The kitchen and dining areas (left) show how the designers have created warm spaces that are not incompatible with a modern spirit. Black is a recurrent color both in the town house and its furnishings (right).

WILLIAM KENTRIDGE
THE REFUSAL OF TIME
VITAMIN
P2
Gerhard Richter | Panorama
THE VICTORIAN VISION

29

Brooklyn Town House

Architects **Roman and Williams**
Location **Brooklyn, New York** Year **2013**

In 2012, the clients for this project, Tracy Martin, CEO of the Morbid Anatomy Museum in Brooklyn, and Vince Clarke, a founding member of the group Depeche Mode, bought a small nineteenth-century brownstone in Park Slope, a largely residential area in Brooklyn known for its historic architecture. Roman and Williams were asked to do away with the modern and minimalist design style of the interiors to return to "a more textured, layered aesthetic hearkening back to the home's roots." The clients suggested that a darker and more feminine aesthetic would be appropriate. Furnishings include a custom-made darkened wood dining table with an eclectic mixture of chairs from Provence and Amsterdam. Worn club chairs, a Berber carpet, and a buffalo hide draped over a black leather sofa set the tone for the 4,000-square-foot (371-square-meter) residence. Custom wallpaper is used on the upper level, with the master bedroom painted entirely in a deep eggplant color and furnished with an 1850s Indian four-poster bed. A Louis XVI daybed and a vintage Aubusson rug are also used to great effect. The feeling of age and wear is carried over into every element of the design, including the bath and kitchen fixtures. Unexpected objects and prints from the collection of the owners are also in tune with the atmosphere, which is very much in keeping with the age of the town house itself. The eclecticism of the design and the furnishings may indeed be what most marks it as a fundamentally contemporary interpretation.

The owners' collection of objects and works of art, together with carefully chosen furniture, gives a lived-in atmosphere to the town house, not typical of architecturally sophisticated spaces.

Lucian Freud
Jay DeFeo
BOTANICALS

Comfort and the clearly expressed presence of culture, both historic and artistic, animate the space (left). Ample natural light flows in through the traditional double windows.

The owners' objects, though of-en unusual, are always imbued with a sense of form and an evocation of the past, which is the leitmotif of the design (right).

30

Mountauk House

Architects **Roman and Williams**
Location **Montauk, New York** Year **Ongoing**

This “relatively unremarkable 1950s ‘contractor special’ with a 1980s addition” might not have seemed the most likely place for a couple of talented New York designers to create a weekend getaway. When asked to give a completion date for this project, the firm responds, “Never, because [principals] Robin [Standefer] and Stephen [Alesch] are always making adjustments and changes to their home and property.” Standefer and Alesch founded Roman and Williams, named after their grandfathers, in New York in 2002. The firm was the 2014 winner of the National Design Award for Interior Design. They say, “At Roman and Williams, we are interested in spaces and objects that people can truly use and things that genuinely last. We are devoted to rebelling against disposability and the common stereotypes about what it means to be ‘modern’ today.” Rather than totally renovating the 1,795-square-foot (167-square-meter) Montauk house, Roman and Williams focused more on the atmosphere of the place than on its physical limitations. Additions did include new wood windows, doors, and walls, and work was done on the exterior landscaping. As is the case in much of the firm’s work, an eclectic spirit is evident. Also evident is their skill at creating spaces that are inviting in addition to being visually and even sensually attractive. The duo’s own description of the interiors emphasizes that quality: “The furnishings are equal parts indulgent luxury and laidback surfer cool. The Danish buffalo leather sofa, draped in angora and indigo, invites post-surf snoozes. The rosewood Sergio Rodrigues table, outfitted with Ted Muehling candlesticks, encourages all manner of dinner party revelry. Robin’s Banque de France desk holds a hippopotamus skull purchased from a bone dealer in Paris, while Stephen’s hand-painted surfboards can be found around the property. Dragging sand into the house is welcomed, and evenings are candlelit and filled with friends, sparks from the backyard fire pit floating up against a summer moon.”

As in other designs by Roman and Williams, there is an obvious relation to the past in the spaces and objects of the house, all of which is orchestrated in a modern way.

Warmth and a succession of different materials, and even different types of wood, are the hallmarks of these spaces, where comfort in the context of eclectic taste is the guiding principle.

31
Villa Vals

Architects **SeARCH**
Location **Vals, Switzerland** Year **2008**

The small village of Vals in the mountains of Switzerland's Graubünden region is well known to architecture fans because of the presence of Peter Zumthor's thermal baths (1996). When the Amsterdam firm SeARCH, led by Bjarne Mastenbroek, was asked to design a house within view of the Zumthor building, it was clearly faced with a difficult challenge. The 2,433-square-foot (226-square-meter) house the team imagined is inserted into the hillside in such a way as to render the residence nearly invisible from the baths. Aside from the nearby building, the architects had to take into account the light and views that this largely underground house would afford its owners. A central patio radiates from the large round opening that constitutes the glazed façade of the house. The architects state, "The local authority's ... planners were pleased that the proposal did not appear 'residential,' nor did it impose on the adjacent baths building. The scheme was not perceived as a typical structure, but rather as an example of pragmatic, unobtrusive development in a sensitive location. The placement of the entrance vis-à-vis an old Graubünder barn and an underground tunnel further convinced them that the concept, while slightly absurd, could still be permitted." The house is made up of an unusual mixture of elements, including a stone façade, concrete, wood, and generous wood-framed glazing. This composition of eclectic materials created in a context where local conservatism meets one of the icons of contemporary architecture (the neighboring Zumthor building) results in an interior that in many ways sums up the spirit of the times.

In a very unusual architectural gesture, in part inspired by the proximity of Peter Zumthor's iconic Vals Baths building, the house is visible only in the form of this largely buried circle of stone.

dutchtub

656

Although the interiors make it evident that the house is largely buried (left), the décor, including a long wooden dining table and quirky light fixtures (right), enliven the space and underline its thoroughly modern qualities.

32

Pringiers Town House

Architects **Glenn Sestig**
Location **Brussels, Belgium** Year **2012**

The Rue aux Laines in Brussels is one of the city's most sought after residential addresses. It is located in the Sablon district in the historic upper area of the Belgian capital. The main public or gallery space of this row house is located on the ground and second floors; the private areas, including the master bedroom and space for guests, are on the three upper floors. The architect explains, "Working within the limitation of a protected façade, the design scoops out the interior completely and transforms it into white, light-filled volumes to maximize the amount of space. Full-height windows in the back look out onto the beautiful green space of Egmont Park." The central element of the interior is a sculptural spiral black metal staircase that intentionally contrasts with the white walls. The ground-floor kitchen has a central element made of gray basaltino that is used to welcome visitors to the gallery space. The town house was shortlisted for the 2014 World Interiors News Annual Awards in the residential category. Sestig was born in 1968 in Ghent. After graduating from the Henry Van De Velde Institute in Antwerp, in 1999 he established his practice together with the Belgian painter Bvardk. Early commissions included shops and showrooms in Ghent, Antwerp, and Brussels, art galleries for the jewelry artist Caroline Van Hoek and others in Brussels and Ghent, as well as nightclubs, houses, and penthouses.

The challenge here consisted of inserting modern, geometric volumes into a more traditional context. The architect succeeds in respecting the environment while being radically modern.

The interiors, seen here before they were occupied, are replete with special visual surprises, including a dark spiraling stairway (left) and framed views (right).

33

Sestig Town House

Architects **Glenn Sestig**
Location **Ghent, Belgium** Year **2013**

Originally built as a private house in the early nineteenth century and used as the home and office of an architect in the 1930s, this town house is located in the heart of Ghent, near Citadel Park. The form of the residence is unusual because it has a round façade facing the corner where it is located. The façade was left essentially intact, with some windows made smaller, whereas the interior was "entirely transformed and reconverted from separate flats into a single cozy and warm winter house." A terrace and pavilion were added to the roof of the house. The key challenge, according to the architects, was "creating a new flow by harmonizing the front and back rooms." The main architectural challenge of the project lies in the long, narrow shape of the house, which is just 15 feet (4.5 meters) wide and 65 feet (20 meters) deep. This limitation was dealt with inside by installing a series of dark gray mirrors. The existing interior was completely stripped out and a new plan was created within the existing house façades, which were renovated and covered with plaster using traditional techniques to maintain the authentic feeling of the building. To complicate matters further, the long house has two separate entrances. The main entrance opens into the central foyer and main stairway. Downstairs, there is a guest area and a small personal spa. The living area faces the curved front of the house and retains the original fireplace. An open kitchen and dining area are accessible from the interior or from the second, everyday entrance. The upper floor houses the master bedroom and dressing area, as well as a bathroom. A new rooftop deck was also part of the project. Glenn Sestig used wood, natural stone, and Moroccan *tadelakt* (a traditional plaster wall coating) to give a warm and natural feeling to the interiors. The majority of the ceilings are painted in various shades of black. On the lower level, where the ceiling height is just over 7 feet (2.2 meters) the ceilings are brighter to create surfaces that reflect light. The floor area of the town house is 4,338 square feet (403 square meters).

The town house is decorated in a contrast of dark and light surfaces with simple furnishings and filtered natural light.

Natural light falls onto opaque surfaces from above. The architect clearly enjoys the contrast in materials offered by the old brick walls and the added plaster, concrete, and black furnishings.

34

House on the Mediterranean

Architects **Álvaro Siza Vieira**
Location **Mallorca, Spain** Year **2008**

Siza's mastery of modern forms is not based on strict grid arrangements. Here, angles and changes in materials appear, from the stone floors and stairs to the white plaster walls.

Built on a steep slope 85 feet (26 meters) above the Mediterranean, this house in many ways sums up all of the art of the architect Álvaro Siza Vieira. Although his forms are white and essentially geometric, the house has an almost organic feeling about it. According to the architect, "Inspired by the surrounding rugged landscapes, the building was planned in a fragmented volumetric composition to unfold as one descends toward the water level. These building volumes consist of three major blocks and are further subdivided into smaller parts. Consisting of two floors and a basement, each volume is arranged as a response to the topography. They are integrated with one another via the platform at 72 feet (22 meters) above sea level." The eastern portion of the composition contains the main entrance, the main and guest bedrooms, and a stairway. The western volume of the residence connects the eastern and northern blocks and contains three bedrooms, a living room, and a patio. The northern block contains the caretaker's residence, with two bedrooms and a living room. The entire house has a floor area of 6,178 square feet (574 square meters). The plot is about 0.9 acre (3,587 square meters). As is often the case, the architect has taken an active interest in the interior of this house, contrasting white plaster, wooden flooring, and stone steps with simple wood furniture. Siza is a master of light and space, and as this house shows, there is an intimate relationship between his architectural designs and their interior finishes.

Windows often frame specific views, and natural light mingles with modern white spaces in the interiors (left). The angled forms of the house on its rocky, pine-covered site are typical of Siza's designs (right).

The exterior angles and orientation of the house are part of an overall scheme that takes into account the site, the views, and the interior design.

35

D10

Architects **Werner Sobek**
Location **Biberach an der Riss, Germany** Year **2010**

Located in Biberach an der Riss, in southern Germany, D10 is a single-story one-family home built in a residential area. Two parallel walls and generous glazing establish the limits of the house. The flat roof of the residence extends beyond the walls, protecting the generous patio area. Together with the glazing, this element of the design "serves to unite the indoor space with the outdoor space." Living areas are on the ground floor, with ancillary spaces in the basement. A two-car garage that can be accessed directly from the basement is located on the northern side of the house. A stairway in the living room of the 1,937-square-foot (180-square-meter) house provides access to the lower level. A geothermal system and a very efficient heat pump provide the energy required to produce hot water and to meet heating and cooling needs. The entire surface of the roof is fitted with a photovoltaic system that generates more power on average annually than the building consumes. This house can clearly trace its origins back to such works as the Farnsworth House by Ludwig Mies van der Rohe (Plano, Illinois, 1951), which also presented itself as a kind of glass box suspended between planar horizontal surfaces. As it happens, Werner Sobek served as the Mies van der Rohe Professor at the Illinois Institute of Technology from 2008 to 2014. In this instance, however, Sobek's knowledge of light structures and his ongoing interest in energy savings have taken the minimal concept of his predecessor several steps further. The interior of this glass house is sparsely furnished, just as Mies might have imagined, but here the connection between interior and exterior becomes more direct and transparent in every sense of the word.

Werner Sobek has long generated forms that rival those of an earlier master, Ludwig Mies van der Rohe, where extreme linear simplicity is combined with lightness and very generous glazing.

Inside, simple surfaces bathed in natural light are orchestrated in a harmonious composition, with a palette of white, gold, and brown.

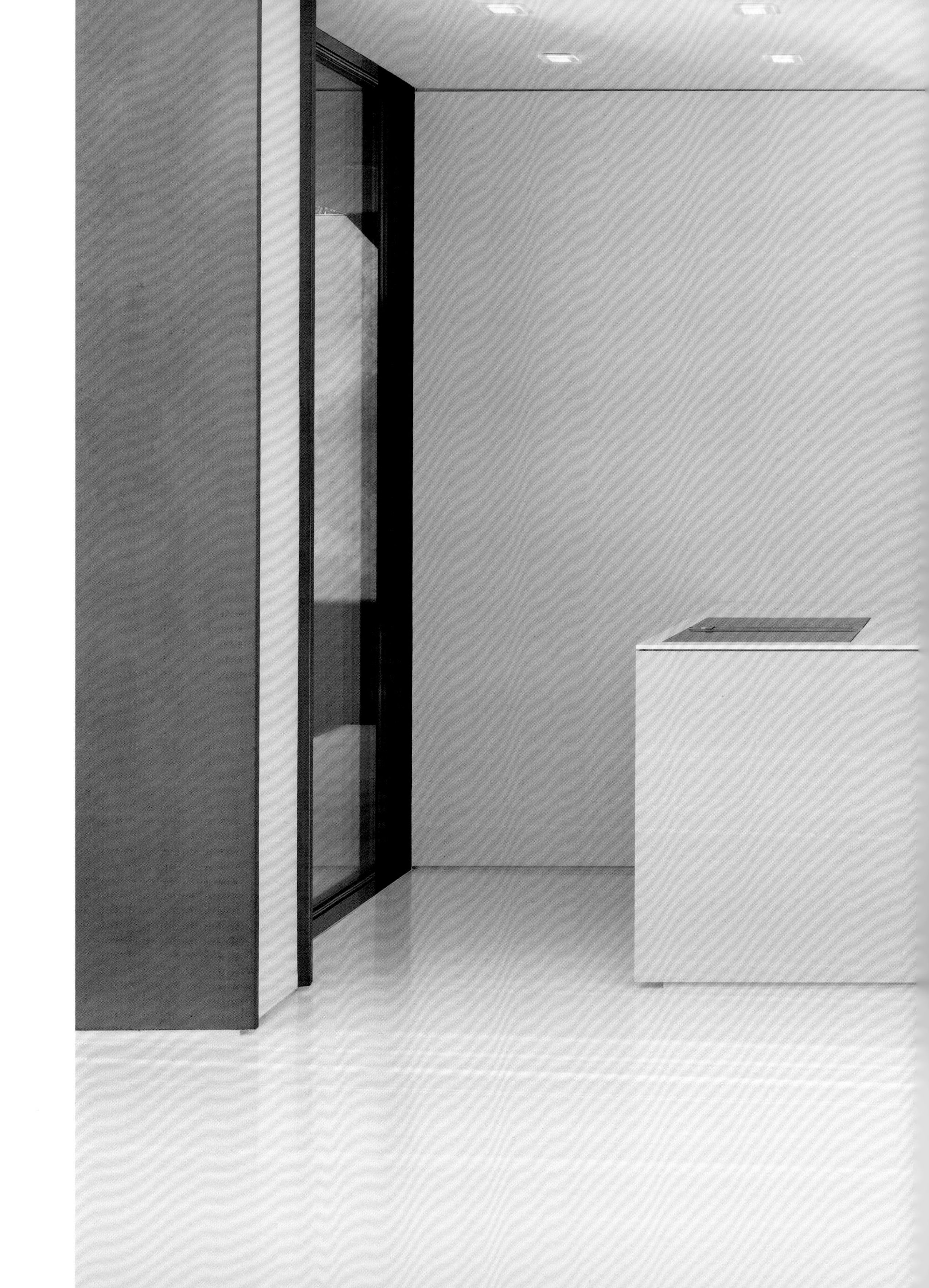

SCHOLPP

36

B10 House

Architects **Werner Sobek**
Location **Stuttgart, Germany** Year **2014**

The Weissenhof Estate in Stuttgart was built for the Deutscher Werkbund exhibition in 1927. Under the direction of Ludwig Mies van der Rohe, the project, which was meant to show what life might be like in the future, included works by Le Corbusier, Walter Gropius, J.J.P. Oud, Bruno Taut, Peter Behrens, and Hans Scharoun, among others. On an unused plot at the same site Werner Sobek built his B10 House, "designed to demonstrate how innovative materials, construction, and technology can sustainably improve our built-up world." Sobek's calculations show that, using sustainable sources, the house can generate twice as much energy as it consumes. Part of an e-mobility showcase funded by the German government, the house will provide power for two electric cars and also for a Le Corbusier-designed house that has been home to the Weissenhof Museum since 2006. The B10 House is slated to be "deconstructed" after three years. The house was designed to be dismantled in one day and rebuilt in the same time frame. Directly after its completion, the house will be opened to visitors as a model of energy concepts and building technologies; at a later time, two students will live there free of charge. Since energy concepts often perform somewhat less well than hoped, the house's energy consumption will be continuously monitored and scientifically analyzed by the University of Stuttgart. Sobek was responsible for the design, general planning, interface design, and sustainability consultancy for this project. With its simple rectangular layout and large glazed surfaces, the B10 House is in keeping with other works by Sobek, who has always been interested in energy-related issues. Furnishings are simple, and the flat surfaces of the interior are covered in oriented strand board, stretched fabric, and linoleum.

The house, perhaps inspired by the model of shipping containers, is lowered into place by a crane onto a pre-installed base, emphasizing its simplicity and low environmental impact.

electric drive
Mein Haus kann mehr. Schon erlebt?
www.aktivhaus-b10.de
02

The principle of the design is that it should generate enough electricity to power not just this house but also another building and two electric cars. Interiors are simple, as are the high, sliding glass doors.

37

Palmyra House

Architects **Studio Mumbai**
Location **Nandgaon, India** Year **2007**

This two-story weekend house is located in a coconut grove in a fishing village called Nandgaon, south of Mumbai. The name of the house is derived from the shading louvers on both volumes, made from local palmyra palms. The house combines an ain wood structure and local basalt for walls, plinths, and paving with plaster finishes whose tone comes from sand found on the site. Three artesian wells provide water, making the whole project ecologically sound and well integrated into its natural environment. Obviously, the warm climate makes such an open house feasible, but the architects have also taken into account natural ventilation and used as many local materials as possible. Combining those aspects with sophisticated, modern techniques, they have succeeded where many others have failed, creating a residential model that is both indigenous and modern. With a total floor area for the two volumes of 3,230 square feet (300 square meters), the house is generous without being the least bit pretentious—a fact that is of note in a time when much more luxurious residences are the norm. Studio Mumbai is one of the more talked-about firms to have emerged from the subcontinent recently. It is led by Bijoy Jain, born in Mumbai in 1965 and educated at Washington University in St. Louis.

The architects combined local traditions with their own knowledge of modernity on an international scale in their design for this house.

The two rectangular blocks, open on the ends, are separated by a reflecting pool. The warm climate allows for window and door panels to be completely open, so the inside can be literally outdoors.

Folding louvered doors make it possible to open the interior almost entirely to the outside. Only the elegant, low rectangular pool separates the two structures, where air flows through naturally, obviating the need for air-conditioning.

Seen either during the day or at night, the volumes of the house appear to open almost entirely. While artificial light brings a warm glow from the inside at night, in daylight the buildings seem to consist of little more than open frames.

38
Integral House

Architects **Shim-Sutcliffe Architects**
Location **Toronto, Canada** Year **2009**

Built in a wooded ravine in the Rosedale neighborhood within view of downtown Toronto, this unusual house includes space for music and performance. According to the architects, "Curvilinear, undulating glass walls with syncopated oak fins are used to shape a large gathering space where building and landscape are intertwined. The journey through the house parallels the experience of descending the ravine slope, taking advantage of the sectional qualities of the site and amplifying the journey through the project." The client, an author of textbooks on mathematics, asked the architects for "curves and performance space" as part of the design. In this instance, the performance space is in fact a 150-seat concert hall. The five-story residence also includes a stairway designed by the glass artist Mimi Gellman and the structural engineer David Bowick, in collaboration with the architects. It is made of hand-blown blue glass and stainless steel cables. There are undulating wood surfaces inside the house, and full-height glazing is generously employed, offering many views of the wooded site. Double-height spaces are also a feature of the design, emphasizing the impression of open space. The main materials employed in the construction of this 15,000-square-foot (1,393-square-meter) residence are concrete, white oak, bronze, glass, and limestone. Glenn D. Lowry, director of New York's Museum of Modern Art, told the *Wall Street Journal* that he believes this is one of the most important private houses built in North America in a number of years.

In the context of a very large and complex house, the architects allow the natural environment to flood the interior with light and views of the surrounding greenery.

An interior staircase (left) assumes a more material presence with its blue coloring. A covered swimming pool (right) opens to the forest, whose forms and colors are reflected in the water.

39

House on Henry's Meadow

Architects **Shim-Sutcliffe Architects**
Location **Vale Perkins, Canada** Year **2009**

The architects state, "This project is located between three distinct landscapes—meadow, lake, and forest. The house is defined by a stacked log wall, a reflecting pool, and low stone retaining walls. Wooden light coffers illuminate the interior spaces, which open up to reveal panoramic views of the lake beyond. The lake and panoramic views can be seen from inside the residence. The stacked log walls are part of the local Quebec agrarian landscape, and this vernacular element is abstracted and integrated in this project." Located on Lake Memphremagog, near the border between Vermont and Quebec, this is the 2,865-square-foot (266-square-meter) vacation house of Glenn D. Lowry, director of the Museum of Modern Art in New York. Indeed, the logs stacked the way firewood is traditionally stored in the area give it the look more of a farm building than of a holiday hideaway. Because of the sloped site, the western and eastern façades of the building are quite different, with large windows facing the lake opposite the log-covered elevation. The north and south faces of the house are clad in painted wood siding. Entry is gained by passing through the log façade, where a vertical slot offers views into the residence. Light is brought into the lower level through a clerestory window. The main living areas are finished with local white pine boards. The stacked log wall allows afternoon light to filter into the house and also creates an unusual pattern when the house is viewed from the outside at night. Aside from an old wooden dining table that faces the lake, the sophisticated and modern furnishings and interiors contrast with the stacked logs and the overall feel of this rural area.

The façade of the house is made up of sawed logs, much like those in local log-storage facilities; a pond is just one element in a sophisticated succession of materials leading up to the house.

Inside (left), wood and glazed surfaces make for a surprisingly modern environment. The house flows from within at night (right) and almost appears to float in its natural environment.

ROUTE
66
DUBAI

40

Houssein Apartment

Architects **Triptyque**
Location **São Paulo, Brazil** Year **2006**

Houssein Jarouche is the Lebanese-Brazilian founder of the concept store MiCasa. In 2005, he asked the architects at the firm Triptyque to redesign his 3,230-square-foot (300-square-meter) apartment in São Paulo. (Triptyque also designed the MiCasa store in that Brazilian city.) The client was looking for a gallery space with aligned rooms not dedicated to any specific function. The architects started by clearing the space, creating a dialogue between the kitchen, the unusual bookcases, and the gallery space. The bookcases, called Treme Treme, enclose the building's elevators and stairs and are present throughout the apartment. Rough concrete, wood recovered from other locations for the floors, stainless steel, and white walls are the basic surface elements. Triptyque cites as an inspiration the French artist Dominique Gonzalez-Foerster and her definition of the tropical identity as "something organic, intense, sensorial, vegetal, pulsating, immature, and out of control." Indeed, the colorful elements are provided not by the architectural design, but by the works of art and pieces of furniture selected by Jarouche. "These colors are a reflection of my personality," he says. "I collect objects I buy when I'm abroad, things from my childhood, and gifts people give me. I love mixing them. I like keeping close everything that is important to me. This is my lifestyle." Furniture by Patricia Urquiola, Charles and Ray Eames, and Konstantin Grcic was also selected by the client, whose MiCasa markets such items. Jarouche insists that he was not motivated by particular combinations of artworks and furniture, and instead says, "The truth is that at my place I do not combine art pieces with furniture or other objects. I'm not interested if they are good or bad or beautiful; they just have to mean something to me. So everything happens in a natural way."

Inside the apartment, an angled wall accommodates a television or books and other objects. Designer furniture is found throughout the residence.

The angled, billowing wall runs through the space like a leitmotif, but the real "stars" of the apartment are the furnishings. Floors made of natural wood bring warmth to the otherwise entirely modern and basically white residence.

41

Casas del Horizonte

Architects **Cristián Undurraga**
Location **Zapallar, Chile** Year **2009**

Zapallar is an elite seaside resort on the central coast of Chile. These two residences are set on a steep slope 82 feet (25 meters) above the Pacific Ocean. The site offers views of the ocean and, on a clear day, of the port of Valparaíso 37 miles (60 kilometers) to the south. The architect, Cristián Undurraga, made a conscious effort not to impose these houses, each of which measures than 4,600 square feet (430 square meters) in floor area, on the already spectacular landscape. Rather, he chose to focus on what he calls the "length" and "magnitude" of the buildings "as a strategy to integrate the sensitivity of the site, covering a length and a magnitude that contains this landscape." Undurraga further explains, "The first field intervention involved the construction of two large cavities whose stone walls are the echo of the rocks that unfold onto lush oceanfront. As a result of this operation, intimate and protected spaces were created on whose walls the houses perch by means of a bridge. These courtyards usher us into a primitive world where the boundaries between architecture and landscape are blurred, while the pavilion/bridges that cross the space and the side facing the water refer to a rational order." The main materials employed in these low, modernist rectangular houses are reinforced concrete, glass, stone, and steel. The ground floor houses the living, dining, and kitchen areas as well as a north-facing patio with a reflecting pond, landscaped with local species of ornamental plants. The bedrooms and bathrooms are upstairs. Concrete is the most visible material both inside and out, with very little ornamentation.

A floating concrete stairway blends easily with the suspended volumes of the house. Broad glazing seems to bring the ocean right into the interior.

The house seen from the beach side (left) consists of broad horizontal planes and, above all, the substantial volume of the flat roof. Inside (right), modernity and a monochrome white palette define the space, which has a concrete ceiling.

42

Haus am Weinberg

Architects **UNStudio**
Location **Stuttgart, Germany** Year **2011**

The architects point out that the very concept of the private home involves a number of paradoxes. Among these is the apparent contradiction between a private interior and a forcibly more public exterior. Even within the house, the overlap between public and private is a delicate, often challenging issue for architects. The location of this house between an old hillside vineyard on one side and a city view on the other adds to this set of inherent incongruities. The organization of the views from inside the house and the distribution of the layout are established by what UNStudio calls "the twist." This central element supports the main staircase as it guides and organizes the flow through the house. The firm explains that the "distribution follows the path of the sun, [so that] each evolution in the twist leads to moments in which views to the outside become an integral experience of the interior." The load-bearing concrete structure was reduced to its minimum expression with the roof and floor slabs supported by the elevator shaft, two pillars, and one inner column. All four corners of the house are glazed and column-free. The residence is approached from the south level, which contains the entrance hall, as well as a garage, wine cellar, guest suite, and diagonal staircase leading upstairs. A double-height glazed corner serves as the dining area and offers broad views to the northwest that frame the vineyard hill. The glass panes at the corner of the house can be fully opened. The living room also sits in a glazed corner, looking southwest. A gallery space is located on the second floor, as is the master bedroom suite and a wellness space. Natural oak flooring, natural stone, and white clay stucco walls with small fragments of reflective stone are used for interior surfaces. Custom features and furnishings are also integrated to blend with and accentuate the architecture. The architects explain, "A white kitchen table/work surface extends from the kitchen to the garden terrace, mimicking the curves in the architecture and further accentuating the connection between the inside and the outside." A dark wood multi-purpose room contrasts with the largely white interiors; it is used as a music room and a display space for hunting trophies.

e architects are masters of computer-
signed, flowing surfaces. The dining
ea sits at the base of an outdoor
rrace and bank of grass.

The staircase (left) seems to emerge from the walls and drip into the lower level. A large table designed by the architects (right) is presided over by somewhat incongruous animal heads.

MALEVICH
OUT OF

43

Art Collector's Loft

Architects **UNStudio**
Location **New York, New York** Year **2010**

This existing loft in the Greenwich Village area of Manhattan "explores the interaction between a gallery and living space, according to the architects. "The main walls in the loft flow through the space, and together with articulated ceilings create hybrid conditions in which exhibition areas merge into living areas." The long, wide space of the loft had relatively low ceilings. The architects introduced flowing curved walls to divide the main space, which had the added benefit of contributing considerable space for hanging works of art. Bookshelves and display cases are part of the design of this wall as well. Ceilings range from luminous to opaque, with the opaque sections intended to disguise the real ceiling height. The luminous sections are backlit by 18,000 LEDs. Views from the loft are emphasized by floor-to-ceiling glazing and a glass balcony that looks toward downtown Manhattan. Partly double-curved glass fiber reinforced gypsum paneling was used for the new wall. Technical installations like HVAC and lighting were integrated into the curved wall elements. The entire floor of the loft is covered in 18-inch (46-centimeter) wide Douglas fir planks. The architects state, "The subtle, even-toned floor unifies the space and allows furniture and art to be positioned as floating elements in changeable constellations." The loft has a net floor space of 4,726 square feet (439 square meters). UNStudio has long experimented with the use of computer-driven design and flowing forms that challenge the more rectilinear ideals of earlier architecture. Here, complex curves and materials literally redefine the shape of this loft's interior to meet the needs of the owner.

The interior of the apartment, with its flowing shelves and bookcases, seems to be one continuous space, into which even the overhead light fixtures are integrated.

Ceilings and walls flow together, creating this partially toplit exhibition space within the house, where light floors and white surfaces allow the artworks to stand out.

MERCURY-TIME
6 YEARS OF 116 DAYS
=696.
JUPITER-TIME
IONIC ORDER
40 YEARS OF 400½ DAYS.
A DAY-FEAST EVERY 4 YEARS IS CELEBRATED AT THE TEMPLE.
PRECESSION OF THE EQUINOXES

44

Casa Cubo

Architects **Isay Weinfeld**
Location **São Paulo, Brazil** Year **2011**

Like a number of other houses in this book, Casa Cubo was designed to serve more than one function. In this instance, the clients, who are art collectors, wanted to create both a residence and a support center for artists and the development of the arts. The architect proposed a cubic block, split into three levels and a mezzanine. The service core is located at the front of the ground level and includes a kitchen, a bathroom, a dining room, and an entrance hall. A generous event space/lounge with a double-height ceiling and polished concrete floors opens onto the back yard. The mezzanine of the lounge, set on the slab atop the service core on the ground floor, houses the library, which is marked by a shelving unit along the entire back wall, a strip of fixed glass next to the floor, and a spiral staircase clad in wood that leads to the private quarters upstairs. These consist of three bedrooms and a living room lit with a floor-to-ceiling opening. The garage and service areas are located in the basement. At 7,675 square feet (713 square meters), the house is larger in area than the plot of land it inhabits, which measures 6,609 square feet (614 square meters). As is the case in many houses by Isay Weinfeld, an emphasis is placed on openness so that the house appears to blend interior and exterior seamlessly. The Brazilian climate naturally facilitates this type of interplay. Weinfeld is a noted master of Brazilian architecture, second only in reputation to such figures as Niemeyer and Mendes da Rocha.

A living space with a ceiling-mounted artwork opens freely into the surrounding garden.

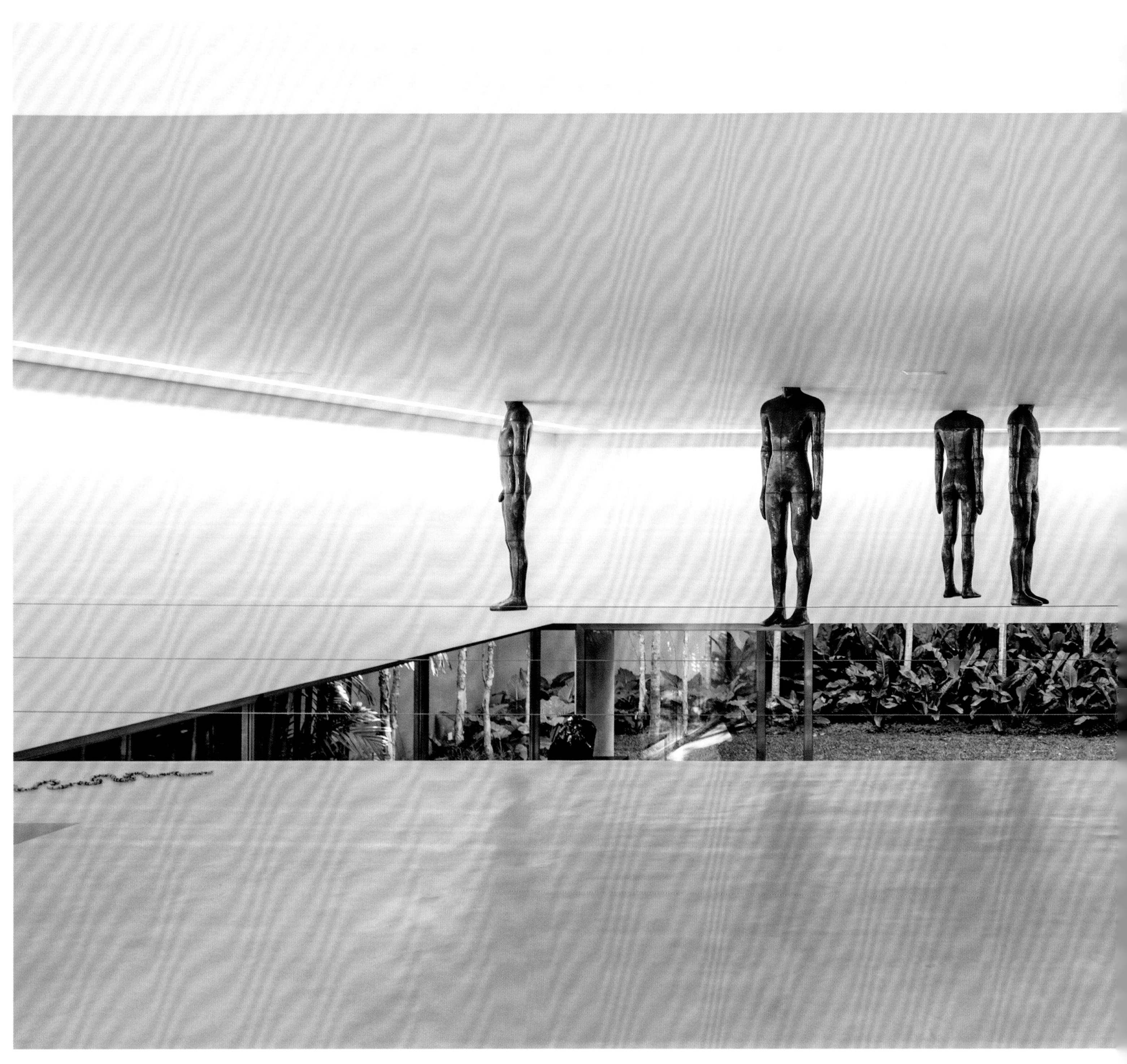

The volume of the house appears to be far heavier in its upper reaches (left) than in the fully glazed ground-floor living area (right).

45

Casa Yucatán

Architects **Isay Weinfeld**
Location **São Paulo, Brazil** Year **2010**

This residence is located in the Jardim América area of Brazil's largest city and was designed for a young couple and their three children. The clients wanted both close contact with nature and the opportunity to show works from their collection of contemporary art. The composition is made up of seven boxlike volumes of different sizes and looks, distributed in an asymmetric pattern. The garage is contained in a black-painted aluminum-clad volume, while another volume holds the kitchen, and yet another houses the dining space. The remaining four blocks contain, respectively, a bedroom for the couple's daughter, a guest room, the master bedroom, and a television room and gym. The architect, Isay Weinfeld, explains, "The 'scattered' layout leaves generous spaces between the volumes that, topped by a wood-covered ceiling slab, not only serve as circulation, but also shelter the main living room, the family room, and the works of art." The rectilinear design provides for direct contact with the densely planted green areas around the house, which is flanked by a pool that extends from the dining area. In the living room, reclaimed wood is used for the floors and ceilings, while the walls are in fair-faced concrete. Furnishings include a pair of walnut lounge chairs designed by George Nakashima with original Jack Lenor Larsen leaf-print velvet upholstery and vintage solid walnut side tables. In the dining room the floor is polished concrete, the walls are white-painted plaster, and the ceiling is white painted gypsum. The dining table was designed by Jorge Zalszupin and the chairs by Hans Wegner. A sideboard was designed by Weinfeld.

The architect uses a carefully orchestrated combination of wood floor and ceiling panels, a stone step, and works of art to animate the interior space seen here.

An interior gallery area combines a concrete floor, plaster wall, dark wooden wall, and overhead lighting to focus attention on the works.

A series of concrete arches covers a garden space (left), while the exterior brings plants and a band of water into contact with the architecture. A sunken seating area (right) is surrounded by high, suspended bookshelves.

AR ODAY

SPEC MIX
Pre-Blended Dry Mortar
TYPE-S

46

Venice House

Architects **wHY**
Location **Los Angeles, California** Year **2012**

As architecture fans know, the Venice neighborhood of Los Angeles is an excellent place to build a house when you are an up-and-coming figure like Kulapat Yantrasast, cofounder and creative director of wHY. Based in Culver City, California, Yantrasast was born in Thailand in 1968 and was a key member of the team of Tadao Ando in Osaka before setting up his own office in the United States. A few blocks inland from Frank Gehry's 1986 Venice Beach house, Yantrasast's 4,305-square-foot (400-square-meter) three-story residence is built around a swimming pool and made primarily with poured-in-place concrete. The architect explains, "The vision of the space is a waterfront—a double-height monolithic concrete cave with views on the south and west sides—which opens onto the water, balancing the minimal yet primitive tectonic of space with an expansive connection to the urban energy of Venice Beach." The actual connection in this instance is more to the Venice streets than to the beach, a situation that the architect rather likes. The entrance is situated on the second floor. Sliding glass doors connect the pool area to the double-height living room that does, indeed, have a cavernlike quality. A guest suite is located on the ground floor and has a porthole window that looks onto the swimming pool. The architect states, "I love concrete. I don't like the idea of cladding a structure with expensive materials like stone or metal. When I came to America, that's what I disliked the most." The house is certainly quirky in both form and décor. A Frank Gehry cardboard chair here, a paper armchair by Tokujin Yoshioka there contribute to what Yantrasast describes as the "D.I.Y." aspects of the house. Additionally, the residence is occupied largely by his own favorite objects, rather than being "decorated" in any traditional sense. "I like the house to be minimal and soulful in its materials and light," Yantrasast says. "But I would not be able to leave it like that without putting in a funny disjunction. Even nature has exceptions."

rchitect, long an important figure in
ffice of Tadao Ando uses a textured
wed wall to animate the main living
; a suspended concrete mezzanine
s as his office space.

The architect uses his talents to the fullest inside the house, creating not only concrete walls, but also an angled counter and a curving staircase.

MARVIS
MALCOLM X
Happy Holidays
Kulepat
SKYSCRAPERS
WINE
LIVING IN STYLE PARIS
WONDERWALL ARCHIVES 01

The house is anything but unremittingly modern, as seen in these shelves full of objects and books, in dark wood (left) and in white-painted wood (right).

Learning from Tadao Ando's use of concrete as a noble material, the architect gives texture and grace to his walls (left). The ground-floor living area opens entirely to the large pool in front of the house (right); an enormous window above, near the architect's study, also looks down on the pool.

47

Lyon House

Architects **Jean-Michel Wilmotte**
Location **Lyon, France** Year **2009**

Jean-Michel Wilmotte has long worked on residential interiors and furniture design in addition to doing his perhaps more publicized work on museum interiors—for the Louvre, the Doha Museum of Islamic Art, and, most recently, the Rijksmuseum in Amsterdam. This rather grand building is an eighteenth-century *hôtel particulier* (large private residence) in the Presqu'île area of Lyon. The 45,391-square-foot (4,217-square-meter) floor area is divided between a residence and, in the eastern wing of the building, offices for the owner, a well-known French businessman. An underground parking area for fifteen cars and a 75-foot (23-meter) swimming pool are among the lower-level elements of the project. The main entrance is on the left side of the courtyard. Ground-floor spaces include a library, two reception rooms, a dining room and kitchen, and a new, monumental staircase. The woodwork of the reception and dining rooms, which helped the building earn historic monument status, were retained. One flight up, the basic spaces are given over to a series of bedrooms. Floors and other woodwork in the master bedroom are also protected by French historic monument rules. Independently accessible duplex apartments were created on the two uppermost levels of the building. Entirely restored and rebuilt where possible inside, this historic building has taken on a new, modern life through the efforts of Wilmotte, who is always at his strongest when he is bringing together past and present. This project was particularly delicate because of the rules governing work on historic monuments, and yet it was ambitious, given the client's needs.

ean-Michel Wilmotte is a master at ransforming historic buildings into odern spaces, as this suspended glass nd stone stairway shows. Colors range rom beige to dark brown and impart quiet elegance.

Wilmotte brings in touches of modernity through furnishings, works of art, a sophisticated lighting system (left), and in a kitchen-dining area and master bedroom (right).

An indoor swimming pool has been added to the old house with an obvious attention to quality and respect for the historic context, yet it is also clearly imbued with modernity.

5

48

Jean-Pierre Raynaud Atelier

Architects **Jean-Michel Wilmotte**
Location **Barbizon, France** Year **2009**

This project for Jean-Pierre Raynaud, a well-known French artist, is located in Barbizon, a town outside of Paris known for its close relation to nineteenth-century painting, Impressionism in particular. Jean-Michel Wilmotte rebuilt an existing house on the property, adding a generous enclosed veranda, and also supervised work on the gardens in close collaboration with Raynaud. The veranda faces the forest of Fontainebleau and is seen by the architect as an indirect homage to the many artists who painted nearby in the nineteenth century. Additions made to the original house in the 1960s were removed in an effort to create greater equilibrium. Although Raynaud does not work in a traditional way, this house where he resided occasionally is called his atelier or studio. A second small structure on the property began as a Nordic-style pavilion for the 1939 World's Fair. It was painted black at the request of the artist. Raynaud has always had a keen eye for positioning his own works; inside the atelier, pieces he created are juxtaposed with Oriental antiques. The atelier has a total floor area of 3,015 square feet (240 square meters), including two smaller upstairs areas (on the second and third floors). The smaller pavilion measures 678 square feet (63 square meters). The Wilmotte design also includes 5,112 square feet (475 square meters) of outdoor terraces and a 3,358-square-foot (312-square-meter) reflecting pool.

Works by Jean-Pierre Raynaud bring color into the largely black and white space. A Chinese rug reflects the artist's fascination with that country.

B

An historic pavilion is set on the grounds, painted black by Raynaud and renovated by Wilmotte. The *Pot Doré* (Golden Pot) to the left is a work by Raynaud.

49

A House

Architects **WMR**
Location **Matanzas, Chile** Year **2013**

WMR was cofounded by Felipe Wedeles, Jorge Manieu, and Macarena Rabat in 2005. (The firm name stands for the partners' names.) Based in Santiago, Chile, the firm has made a considerable reputation creating houses along the Chilean coast, often with very limited means. The A House measures just 344 square feet (32 square meters) in floor area and, its name A signifies the search for a form that is cheap and easy to build. A young cousin of Wedeles's told the architects he wanted a "super-low-cost" house, which he volunteered to build himself. Made with pine and plywood two-by-fours with resin employed to waterproof the shower and kitchen deck, the house reflects the same spectacular sensibility that WMR has shown in other projects where they have created a relationship between remarkable coastal sites and a simple style of architecture.

A rough stone wall faces a glazed wall and terrace. Inside, rough wood harmonizes with the stone and also brings a note of warmth.

A broad outdoor terrace is covered by a canopy and offers a splendid view of the ocean. Furnishings are simple and comfortable.

50

Casa Swift

Architects **WMR**
Location **Matanzas, Chile** Year **2014**

The unexpected design of this house stems from the commission. The architects were asked to create rooms that are independent from each other, rather like those in a hotel. The resulting split-level design includes a lower-level swimming pool, a parking area, and a gym on the ground level; bedrooms on an intermediate floor that is connected to the pool level via a ramp; and an open living room and kitchen on the uppermost floor. The house is closed against dominant winds on the south and completely open to the northwest, overlooking the bay. Locally sourced timber and glass are the main elements of the house, which, like others created by WMR, has spectacular views of the Chilean coast and a relatively low construction price. Timber interiors with simple angled supports are a signature of the house, as are simple, largely wooden furnishings. The basic frame of the house and its plan are rectilinear. The architects' innovation is focused on building astonishing houses for budgets that put them within reach of clients who are not very wealthy. Who says a great view requires bundles of cash?

The architects specialize in inventive modern houses on the Chilean coast that are built for relatively low budgets. Here, rough wood and steel form pavilion-like elements that are partially open and partially closed.

Rough wood surfaces and angled pillars form the interiors, where full-height glazing opens onto outdoor decks.

NOTES

1. Mario Botta, interview with the author, Lugano, Switzerland, August 16, 1998.

2. Terence Riley, *The UnPrivate House* (New York: The Museum of Modern Art and Harry N. Abrams, 1999).

3. Niklas Maak, "Ommetaphobia," in *Window, Elements of Architecture* (Venice: Marsilio, 2014).

4. Rem Koolhaas, *Window, Elements of Architecture* (Venice: Marsilio, 2014).

5. Apostolos Mitsios, "Houssein Jarouche's Apartment by Triptyque" (includes an interview with Houssein Jarouche), *Yatzer*, December 30, 2010, www.yatzer.com/Hussein-Jarouche-Apartment-by-Triptyque, accessed on September 1, 2014.

6. Joseph Giovannini, "A Fine Second Act for a Summer House" (includes an interview with Peter Shelton), *Architectural Digest*, July 2008, www.architecturaldigest.com/AD100/2010/shelton_mindel/mindel_article_072008, accessed on September 4, 2014.

7. Tom Wolfe, *From Bauhaus to Our House* (New York: Farrar, Straus and Giroux, 1981).

Page 6. Isay Weinfeld, Casa Cubo, São Paulo, Brazil, 2011

Page 9. HHF, Tsai Residence and Guesthouse, Ancram, New York, 2008/2011

Page 10. Eduardo Arroyo - No.MAD Arquitectos, Zafra-Uceda House, Aranjuez, Spain, 2009

Pages 14–15. Mareines + Patalano Arquitetura, Leaf House, Angra dos Reis, Rio de Janeiro, Brazil, 2008

Pages 16–17. Carlos Ferrater, OAB, AA House, Vallès Occidental, Barcelona, Spain, 2009

Pages 18–19. Shim-Sutcliffe, Integral House, Toronto, Canada, 2009